First Workshop on Learning with Natural Language Supervision (LNLS 2022)

Dublin, Ireland
26 May 2022

ISBN: 978-1-7138-6745-6

Printed from e-media with permission by:

Curran Associates, Inc.
57 Morehouse Lane
Red Hook, NY 12571

Some format issues inherent in the e-media version may also appear in this print version.

Printed with permission by Curran Associates, Inc. (2023)

For permission requests, please contact the Association for Computational Linguistics at the address below.

Association for Computational Linguistics
209 N. Eighth Street
Stroudsburg, Pennsylvania 18360

Phone: 1-570-476-8006
Fax: 1-570-476-0860

acl@aclweb.org

Additional copies of this publication are available from:

Curran Associates, Inc.
57 Morehouse Lane
Red Hook, NY 12571 USA
Phone: 845-758-0400
Fax: 845-758-2633
Email: curran@proceedings.com
Web: www.proceedings.com

LNLS 2022

The First Workshop on Learning with Natural Language Supervision

Proceedings of the Workshop

May 26, 2022

The LNLS organizers gratefully acknowledge the support from the following sponsors.

Gold

DeepMind

Introduction

To a growing extent, advances across machine learning application domains are driven by advances in NLP. In computer vision, image captions are used to shape learned representations of images [Frome et al., 2013, Mu et al., 2020, Radford et al., 2021, Desai and Johnson 2021]. In programming languages, textual code comments are used to guide and constrain models for example-based program synthesis [Yaghmazadeh et al., 2017, Austin et al., 2021, Wong et al., 2021]. In robotics and more general policy learning settings, rules and instructions are used to enable generalization to new environments and goals [Zhong et al., 2020, Narasimhan et al., 2018, Sharma et al., 2020]. Within NLP, rich natural-language annotations and task descriptions are used to improve the performance and interpretability of models for text categorization and question answering [Hancock et al., 2018, Weller et al., 2020, Efrat et al., 2020]. And in cognitive science, experimental evidence suggests that language shapes many other aspects of human cognition (e.g. Jones et al., 1991).

At present, however, most research on learning from language takes place within individual application domains (and mostly outside of the NLP community). While many approaches to language supervision are domain-general, and closely connected to "core" NLP research, there are currently no venues where researchers from across the field can meet to share ideas and draw connections between their disparate lines of research. Our workshop will offer a central meeting point for research on language-based supervision, enabling researchers within and beyond NLP to discuss how language processing models and algorithms can be brought to bear on problems beyond the textual realm (e.g. visual recognition, robotics, program synthesis, sequential decision making). Existing workshops like RoboNLP, SPLU, and ViGiL focus on models for multi-modality; inspired by the relationship between language and human cognitive development, our workshop will emphasize broader use of language not just as an input modality but a fundamental source of information about the structure of tasks and problem domains.

In keeping with this interdisciplinary focus, our workshop format differs in two ways from a standard NLP workshop: first, with a special emphasis on speakers and attendees who would not typically attend NLP conferences; second, by replacing the standard panel discussion with a series of workshop-wide breakout sessions aimed at seeding cross-institutional collaborations around new tasks, datasets, and models.

Organizing Committee

Organizing Committee

Jacob Andreas, MIT, USA
Karthik Narasimhan, Princeton University, USA
Aida Nematzadeh, DeepMind, UK

Program Committee

Program Chairs

Jacob Andreas, Massachusetts Institute of Technology and Microsoft
Karthik R Narasimhan, Princeton University
Aida Nematzadeh, Deepmind

Reviewers

Siddharth Karamcheti, Stanford University
Theodore Sumers, Princeton University
Afra Feyza Akyürek, Boston University
Bishan Yang, Carnegie Melon University
Jesse Mu, Stanford University
Catherine Wong, Massachusetts Institute of Technology
Erin Grant, University of California Berkeley
Ekin Akyürek, Massachusetts Institute of Technology
Pratyusha Sharma, Massachusetts Institute of Technology
Ameet Deshpande, Princeton University
Evan Hernandez, Massachusetts Institute of Technology
Olivia Watkins, University of California, Berkeley
Robert D. Hawkins, Princeton University
Shunyu Yao, Princeton University
Rakesh R Menon, Department of Computer Science, University of North Carolina, Chapel Hill

Table of Contents

Finding Sub-task Structure with Natural Language Instruction

Ryokan Ri[1]
li0123@logos.t.u-tokyo.ac.jp*

Yufang Hou[2]
YHou@ie.ibm.com

Radu Marinescu[2]
radu.marinescu@ie.ibm.com

Akihiro Kishimoto[2]
Akihiro.Kishimoto@ibm.com

[1]The University of Tokyo [2]IBM Research

Abstract

When mapping a natural language instruction to a sequence of actions, it is often useful to identify sub-tasks in the instruction. Such sub-task segmentation, however, is not necessarily provided in the training data. We present the A2LCTC (Action-to-Language Connectionist Temporal Classification) algorithm to automatically discover a sub-task segmentation of an action sequence. A2LCTC does not require annotations of correct sub-task segments and learns to find them from pairs of instruction and action sequence in a weakly-supervised manner. We experiment with the ALFRED dataset and show that A2LCTC accurately finds the sub-task structures. With the discovered sub-tasks segments, we also train agents that work on the downstream task and empirically show that our algorithm improves the performance.

1 Introduction

Building computational agents that execute actions given natural language instruction has a great deal of potential in real-world applications. One common approach is to cast the problem as mapping from instruction text into action sequence, and train an agent with supervised learning (Chen and Mooney, 2011; Mei et al., 2016). A challenge on effective machine learning stems from a long horizon of the tasks. Typical navigation tasks often involve more than a paragraph of instructions (Chen and Mooney, 2011; Misra et al., 2017; Shridhar et al., 2020). In such cases, many existing approaches exploit the task hierarchy, *e.g.*, decompose one episode of the task into sub-tasks and treat them as separate training instances (Mei et al., 2016), incorporate the hierarchical information into the model (Zhu et al., 2020), or aid the learning process with progress monitoring (Ma et al., 2019).

However, annotations for such a decomposition are not necessarily available in training data. In this case, previous work has attempted to perform sub-task segmentation by augmenting data through crowdsourcing (Hong et al., 2020), or developing a heuristic algorithm (Zhu et al., 2020).

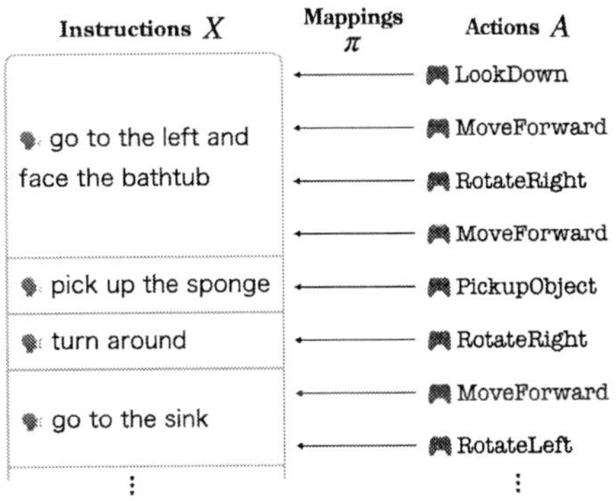

Figure 1: Example illustrating a mapping from each action to a corresponding fine-grained instruction

In this paper, we present A2LCTC (Action-to-Language Connectionist Temporal Classification), an unsupervised algorithm that *automatically* discovers a sub-task segmentation of an action sequence. Given pairs of a natural language instruction and action sequence, A2LCTC maps each action to a fine-grained instruction (Figure 1).

We formulate the problem of sub-task segmentation as classification of each action into a fine-grained instruction. Inspired by the connectionist temporal classification algorithm (Graves et al., 2006), we consider an objective function that maximizes the log-likelihood of the coarsely aligned data. This formulation allows us to learn the classification in a weakly-supervised manner without any need of the ground truth mapping.

We experiment with the ALFRED dataset which involves navigating a robot to perform household task (Shridhar et al., 2020). A2LCTC successfully discovers the sub-task information in the unsegmented training data (§3), which are shown to be useful for the downstream task (§4).

* Work done as an intern at IBM Research.

Proceedings of the First Workshop on Learning with Natural Language Supervision, pages 1 - 9
May 26, 2022 ©2022 Association for Computational Linguistics

2 Learning Sub-task Segmentation

Given a training instance of a navigation task which consists of language instruction X and action sequence $A = [a_1, ..., a_T]$, we aim at finding a decomposition of the instance $(X, A) = [(X_1, A_1), ..., (X_L, A_L)]$, which is semantically plausible and useful for learning the task.

Our approach starts with dividing the instruction into fine-grained segments. In the experiment, the segment X_i corresponds to a verbal phrase (*e.g.*, "*go to the desk*") extracted from the instruction using a simple rule-based algorithm (Appendix A.1).

2.1 Formulating the Task as Temporal Classification

We formulate the decomposition task as classification of actions into one of the fine-grained instructions: our algorithm predicts a mapping $\pi = [\pi_1, ..., \pi_T]$ where $\pi_t \in [1, L]$.

We assume that the alignment is monotonic, *i.e.*, the actions and instructions are both arranged in a chronological order, which typically holds for step-by-step instruction text[1]. This formulation allows us to develop an *unsupervised* learning method to effectively solve the task without ground-truth label mappings. We introduce A2LCTC (Action-to-Language Connectionist Temporal Classification), which is based on the CTC algorithm originally used for speech recognition (Graves et al., 2006) or action labeling in video (Huang et al., 2016).

Our model attempts to maximize the following likelihood for each training instance:

$$\sum_{\{\pi|\mathcal{B}(\pi)=[1,2,..,L]\}} P(\pi|X, A) \qquad (1)$$

where $\mathcal{B}$ is the operator to remove repeated labels, *e.g.*,, $B([1, 1, 2, 2, 2, 3]) = [1, 2, 3]$. That is, the objective is the sum of the probabilities over all the possible assignments under the monotonic constraint. Under the conditional independence assumption, we further decompose the likelihood into $P(\pi|X, A) = \prod_t^T P(\pi_t|X, A)$.
With this decomposition, we employ the forward algorithm (Stratonovich, 1965) to efficiently calculate the sum over all possible paths.

[1]In case that the monotonic assumption does not hold, we could reorder instructions with some sentence-ordering algorithm such as (Ghosal et al., 2021) as preprocessing.

2.2 Modeling with Neural Network

We model the probability computation using neural networks. In our approach, each fine-grained instruction and action are represented as feature vectors. We then define the probability $P(\pi_t|X, A)$ as the softmax of the dot product of the feature vectors of the action $\boldsymbol{a}_t$ and the instruction $[\boldsymbol{x}_1, ..., \boldsymbol{x}_L]$:

$$P(\pi_t = i|X, A) = \frac{\exp(\boldsymbol{a}_t \cdot \boldsymbol{x}_i)}{\sum_{j=1}^{L} \exp(\boldsymbol{a}_t \cdot \boldsymbol{x}_j)}. \qquad (2)$$

In our implementation, a fine-grained instruction X_i is tokenized into words and $\boldsymbol{x_i}$ is computed as the average of the word embeddings followed by a linear layer. The action feature vectors are computed by feeding action embeddings $[\hat{\boldsymbol{a}}_1, ..., \hat{\boldsymbol{a}}_T]$ into a one-layer bidirectional LSTM (Hochreiter and Schmidhuber, 1997) to capture the semantics of actions in the context.

At inference time, the model induces the best mapping π that maximize $P(\pi|X, A)$ with the viterbi algorithm to form decomposed instances (X_i, A_i).

2.3 Stabilization of Unsupervised Learning

Optimizing the aforementioned objective function with neural networks turns out to be highly unstable. Therefore, we further employ the following techniques to better guide the training process.
Length-based curriculum learning. The training objective (1) is defined as the sum of the probabilities over all possible assignments, whose size grows at the speed of $\mathcal{O}(L^T)$. When L and T are large, too many degenerated assignments take up a large part of the probability mass, which hinders the training especially at the beginning of training.

To address this problem, we adopt the curriculum learning framework (Bengio et al., 2009). At the beginning of training, we restrict the training instances with a shorter action sequence and gradually expose the model to longer instances (Spitkovsky et al., 2010). Details are shown in Appendix A.4.
Initializing with pre-trained word embeddings. We initialize the word embeddings $\boldsymbol{w}$ with the Glove embeddings (Pennington et al., 2014) to inject a model with the prior knowledge of words.
Initializing with pre-trained action embeddings. We also initialize the action embeddings $\hat{\boldsymbol{a}}$ with pre-trained embeddings. We obtain action embeddings from the action sequences in the training data with Skip-gram (Mikolov et al., 2013).

3 Experiments

We test A2LCTC with the ALFRED dataset (Shridhar et al., 2020) [2], where the agent performs household tasks in a simulated indoor environment given English instruction. We choose this dataset because (1) the data involves relatively long sequence of actions (over 100); (2) it offers ground-truth sub-task segmentation data which allows the evaluation of our algorithm. Although the ALFRED task itself involves understanding visual inputs, which is currently beyond the scope of A2LCTC, the action set defined in the dataset is semantically rich enough for A2LCTC to solve the segmentation problem.

3.1 Experimental Setups

Training and Evaluation Data. The dataset contains expert demonstrations, which are split into the training set and two validation sets: *valid_seen* and *valid_unseen*. In *valid_seen*, the ALFRED tasks are given in the same set of environments as the training data, while unseen environments are used for *valid_unseen*. We use *valid_seen* as the validation set during training and report the results evaluated with both of them.

The task defines 12 types of actions: five for navigation (e.g., `LookUp`, `MoveForward`, `RotateRight`) and seven for interaction (e.g., `Pickup`, `Slice`). To simplify training and evaluation, we preprocess data by merging the same consecutive navigation actions into a single action (see Appendix B for detailed statistics on the data).

Evaluation Metrics. Each training instance in the ALFRED dataset contains ground-truth sub-goal segments for instructions and actions. We use them to evaluate the learned sub-task segments.

Note that our algorithm operates on finer-grained instructions segmented into verbal phrases, while the ground-truth segments are coarser; some sentences contain a couple of verbal phrases (*e.g.*, "*Rinse the sponge out in the sink, and pick it up again*"). In our evaluation, we first merge the fine-grained instructions into their corresponding sub-goal instruction, together with the mapped actions, and then compare the overlap with the gold sub-goal segments of actions.

We report the sub-goal exact match (EM) score defined as the percentage of the sub-goal segments perfectly reconstructed. We also report the sub-goal F1 score defined as the macro average of the F1 scores calculated by taking the overlap between the predicted and ground-truth segment.

3.2 Baselines

Under our task formulation, A2LCTC offers an advantage that it can take into account the temporal constraint and the semantics of instructions. However, many existing unsupervised sequence alignment algorithms (*e.g.*, IBM models) operate only between discrete symbols and are not directly applicable in this situation where we need to align actions to text (or a bag of words in our model). Thus, we compare A2LCTC with two baselines that do not consider the textual information.

Uniform. The uniform baseline assigns an equal number of actions to each of the fine-grained instructions.

Byte-pair Encoding. The byte-pair encoding (BPE) baseline is based on a data compression algorithm that finds repeated patterns in the data and merges them into chunks (Gage, 1994; Sennrich et al., 2016). Concretely, we repeat the following two steps until each action sequence is split into the number of the corresponding fine-grained instructions: (1) count bigrams in the action sequences; (2) merge the most frequent bigrams.

3.3 Results

Table 1 shows that A2LCTC significantly outperforms the baselines, which indicates that our model successfully leverages textual information and learns meaningful alignments between the fine-grained instructions and actions.

Although the BPE baseline does not use textual information, it exhibits reasonable F1 scores (61.9 points in *valid_unseen* and much higher EM scores than UNIFORM (27.1 vs. 9.3 points). This reflects the characteristics of the ALFRED dataset. As each episode in the dataset is generated from specific templates, the actions follow specific patterns, which enable the BPE to learn correct segmentation to some extent.

3.4 Ablation Study

In A2LCTC, we utilize several techniques to stabilize the training process. Table 2 shows the effects of ablating one stabilization method from the full A2LCTC model. Our results indicate that curriculum learning is most essential to successful training. Without curriculum learning, A2LCTC suffers from significant performance degradation (41.2 → 14.6 in EM and 78.2 → 36.7 in F1 score).

[2] `https://askforalfred.com/`, MIT License

	valid_seen		*valid_unseen*	
	EM	F1	EM	F1
UNIFORM	8.8	54.4	9.3	55.5
BPE	22.8	61.9	27.1	65.9
A2LCTC	**61.2**	**85.3**	**58.5**	**85.1**

Table 1: Performance for sub-task segmentation. The value of A2LCTC is the best among 10 runs with different random seeds.

	EM	F1
Full	41.2 ± 10.2	78.2 ± 10.8
- pre. language	33.5 ± 14.1	70.2 ± 18.0
- pre. action	41.1 ± 13.4	76.9 ± 18.2
- curriculum	14.6 ± 5.7	36.7 ± 8.0

Table 2: Ablation model performance (*valid_seen*). The values show the mean and standard deviation of 10 runs.

Ablating pre-training language or action embeddings still obtains mean values comparable to the full A2LCTC but yields much larger standard deviations. This indicates that these two stabilization methods are also beneficial for A2LCTC.

4 Evaluation with the Downstream Task

We evaluate the effectiveness of sub-task segments induced by A2LCTC on the downstream ALFRED task.

Models. Our baseline agent (BASELINE) is based on the CNN-LSTM sequence-to-sequence architecture in Shridhar et al. (2020), which takes the whole instruction and current state as input and then predicts an action at each time step. Unless specified, we use the same hyperparameters as the original implementation.

To incorporate the sub-task information, we extend the baseline with the progress monitoring module (Ma et al., 2019). We use two progress monitoring schemes from Shridhar et al. (2020), which estimate the current time step and the completed sub-tasks. Specifically, the modules are trained to predict the proportion of elapsed steps or completed sub-tasks to the total numbers.

We evaluate the segmentation of A2LCTC as well as the two baseline methods (UNIFORM and BPE). Those algorithms are applied on the training data and the agents are trained with the progress monitoring according to the segmentation.

Metric. We evaluate the agents with the subgoal sequence accuracy. The agent predicts the next action given the history from an expert trajectory. The metric measures how many subgoal chunks of actions, which is defined by the ground-truth segmentation of the dataset, are successfully predicted in the evaluation data. Note that this metric simplifies the original task in that it ignores the object interactions and focuses on action prediction[3].

	valid_seen	*valid_unseen*
BASELINE	57.6 ± 2.0	29.6 ± 1.5
UNIFORM	63.6 ± 2.5	38.8 ± 1.4
BPE	66.0 ± 2.0	39.1 ± 0.4
A2LCTC	$\mathbf{69.7 \pm 1.4}$	$\mathbf{41.4 \pm 0.8}$

Table 3: Performance on the ALFRED task measured by the subgoal sequence accuracy. The values show the mean and standard deviation of 5 runs.

Results. Table 3 summarizes the result. On both *valid_seen* and *valid_unseen* splits, the agents trained with fine-grained instruction (UNIFORM, BPE and A2LCTC) significantly outperform BASELINE. The fact that UNIFORM achieves improvement indicates that keeping track of detailed progress is helpful even if it inaccurately performs the fine-grained task segmentation (see Section 3.3). A2LCTC performs best because of the better accuracy of the segmentation than the others. This demonstrates that A2LCTC successfully provides more informative instructions for the agent in solving the downstream task.

5 Conclusion

We presented A2LCTC, which finds a hierarchical structure of an action sequence by mapping each action to fine-grained natural language instructions without ground-truth mapping data. We demonstrated that A2LCTC successfully learns meaningful segments and training the ALFRED agents with these segments leads to improved performance.

A2LCTC currently relies only on semantic correspondence between actions and text. Applying A2LCTC to the tasks with low-level actions is an important extension, *e.g.*, actions specifying the direction to move. Furthermore, the instruction may often describe the visual input whose information is not encoded in the actions. Another important future direction is to incorporate visual or additional information to tackle a broader range of domains.

[3]We find the original navigation task is too difficult for the baseline model: the success rate is very low with high variance, which prevents meaningful comparison among the variants of the model (Appendix D).

References

Yoshua Bengio, Jérôme Louradour, Ronan Collobert, and Jason Weston. 2009. Curriculum learning. In *ICML*, volume 382 of *ACM International Conference Proceeding Series*, pages 41–48. ACM.

David L. Chen and Raymond J. Mooney. 2011. Learning to interpret natural language navigation instructions from observations. In *AAAI*.

P. Gage. 1994. A new algorithm for data compression. *The C Users Journal archive*, 12:23–38.

Deepanway Ghosal, Navonil Majumder, Rada Mihalcea, and Soujanya Poria. 2021. Stack: Sentence ordering with temporal commonsense knowledge. In *Proceedings of the 2021 Conference on Empirical Methods in Natural Language Processing (EMNLP)*.

Alex Graves, Santiago Fernández, Faustino J. Gomez, and Jürgen Schmidhuber. 2006. Connectionist temporal classification: labelling unsegmented sequence data with recurrent neural networks. In *ICML*, volume 148 of *ACM International Conference Proceeding Series*, pages 369–376. ACM.

Sepp Hochreiter and Jürgen Schmidhuber. 1997. Long short-term memory. *Neural Computation*, 9(8):1735–1780.

Yicong Hong, Cristian Rodriguez, Qi Wu, and Stephen Gould. 2020. Sub-instruction aware vision-and-language navigation. In *Proceedings of the 2020 Conference on Empirical Methods in Natural Language Processing (EMNLP)*, pages 3360–3376, Online. Association for Computational Linguistics.

De-An Huang, Li Fei-Fei, and Juan Carlos Niebles. 2016. Connectionist temporal modeling for weakly supervised action labeling. In *Computer Vision - ECCV 2016 - 14th European Conference, Amsterdam, The Netherlands, October 11-14, 2016, Proceedings, Part IV*, volume 9908 of *Lecture Notes in Computer Science*, pages 137–153. Springer.

Chih-Yao Ma, Jiasen Lu, Zuxuan Wu, G. Al-Regib, Z. Kira, R. Socher, and Caiming Xiong. 2019. Self-monitoring navigation agent via auxiliary progress estimation. *ArXiv*, abs/1901.03035.

Hongyuan Mei, Mohit Bansal, and Matthew R. Walter. 2016. Listen, attend, and walk: Neural mapping of navigational instructions to action sequences. In *AAAI*.

Tomas Mikolov, Kai Chen, Greg Corrado, and Jeffrey Dean. 2013. Efficient estimation of word representations in vector space. *CoRR*, abs/1301.3781.

Dipendra Misra, John Langford, and Yoav Artzi. 2017. Mapping instructions and visual observations to actions with reinforcement learning. In *Proceedings of the 2017 Conference on Empirical Methods in Natural Language Processing*, pages 1004–1015, Copenhagen, Denmark. Association for Computational Linguistics.

Jeffrey Pennington, Richard Socher, and Christopher Manning. 2014. GloVe: Global vectors for word representation. In *Proceedings of the 2014 Conference on Empirical Methods in Natural Language Processing (EMNLP)*, pages 1532–1543, Doha, Qatar. Association for Computational Linguistics.

Rico Sennrich, Barry Haddow, and Alexandra Birch. 2016. Neural machine translation of rare words with subword units. In *Proceedings of the 54th Annual Meeting of the Association for Computational Linguistics (Volume 1: Long Papers)*, pages 1715–1725, Berlin, Germany. Association for Computational Linguistics.

Mohit Shridhar, Jesse Thomason, Daniel Gordon, Yonatan Bisk, Winson Han, Roozbeh Mottaghi, Luke Zettlemoyer, and Dieter Fox. 2020. Alfred: A benchmark for interpreting grounded instructions for everyday tasks. In *Proceedings of the IEEE/CVF Conference on Computer Vision and Pattern Recognition (CVPR)*.

Valentin I. Spitkovsky, Hiyan Alshawi, and Daniel Jurafsky. 2010. From baby steps to leapfrog: How "less is more" in unsupervised dependency parsing. In *Human Language Technologies: The 2010 Annual Conference of the North American Chapter of the Association for Computational Linguistics*, pages 751–759, Los Angeles, California. Association for Computational Linguistics.

Ruslan Leont'evich Stratonovich. 1965. Conditional markov processes. In *Non-linear transformations of stochastic processes*, pages 427–453. Elsevier.

Wang Zhu, Hexiang Hu, Jiacheng Chen, Zhiwei Deng, Vihan Jain, Eugene Ie, and Fei Sha. 2020. BabyWalk: Going farther in vision-and-language navigation by taking baby steps. In *Proceedings of the 58th Annual Meeting of the Association for Computational Linguistics*, pages 2539–2556, Online. Association for Computational Linguistics.

A Implementation details of A2LCTC

A.1 Instruction Decomposition

We split a whole instruction into fine-grained instructions each of which is a verbal phrase. Our current implementation employs a simple rule-based algorithm, which segments a whole instruction at periods, commas, phrases such as *and* or *then*. For example, "*Turn around and go back to the table*" will be segmented into ["*Turn around*", "*go back to the table*"], while we also write few rules to handle erroneous splits such as conjunctions between nouns (["*take the apple*", "*(and) banana*"]), commas before a prepositional phrase (["*Put the bowl*", "*(,) on the coffee table to the left of the statue*"]), or verbal phrases that cannot be instruction by itself (["*go to the left*", "*(and) face the bathtub*"]).

A.2 Neural Network Architecture

Instruction Feature Vectors

The feature vector of a fine-grained instruction $\boldsymbol{X}_l$ is simply modeled by taking the average of the word embeddings $[\boldsymbol{w}_1, ..., \boldsymbol{w}_N]$ followed by a linear layer (the results from different encoding strategies are shown in Appendix C).

$$\boldsymbol{x} = \tanh(\text{Linear}(\frac{1}{N}\sum_{i}^{N} \boldsymbol{w}_i)). \tag{3}$$

In our experiment, the dimension of word embeddings, the input and output size of the linear layer is all set to 50. The total number of parameters of A2LCTC is about 44K. The training takes approximately one hour with a single GPU.

Action Feature Vectors

The action feature vectors are computed through feeding embeddings for primitive actions $[\hat{\boldsymbol{a}}_1, ..., \hat{\boldsymbol{a}}_T]$ to a one-layer bidirectional LSTM.

$$\boldsymbol{a}_1, ..., \boldsymbol{a}_T = \text{LSTM}(\hat{\boldsymbol{a}}_1, ..., \hat{\boldsymbol{a}}_T) \tag{4}$$

where $[\hat{\boldsymbol{a}}_1, ..., \hat{\boldsymbol{a}}_T]$ are embeddings for primitive actions.

The size of the action embeddings and the hidden size of the LSTM are set to 50. The outputs of LSTM in the forward and backward directions are summed to merged into one single feature vector.

A.3 Hyperparameters for training

optimizer	Adam
learning rate	0.001
batch size	128
validation metric	the sub-goal F1 score
patience	5

A.4 Stabilization of Unsupervised Learning

Length-based curriculum learning

We set the maximum length of training instances for each training epoch according to a schedule. In our experiment, the maximum length starts at 20, and linearly increases to 60 with 30 steps.

Initializing with pre-trained action embeddings

We use the `gensim` library[4] to train action embeddings. We use the Skip-gram algorithm and the hyperparameters are shown in Table 4

[4]https://radimrehurek.com/gensim/

embedding size	50
window size	1
# of iterations	15
# of negative samples	5

Table 4: The hyperparameters for training action embeddings

B Data Statistics

Our experiments are based on the expert demonstration data in the ALFRED dataset (Table 5).

training data	valid_seen	valid_unseen
21,023	820	821

Table 5: The number of expert demonstrations in the ALFRED dataset.

After the instruction decomposition, the instructions contain 10 fine-grained instructions on average. The entire distribution is shown in Figure2.

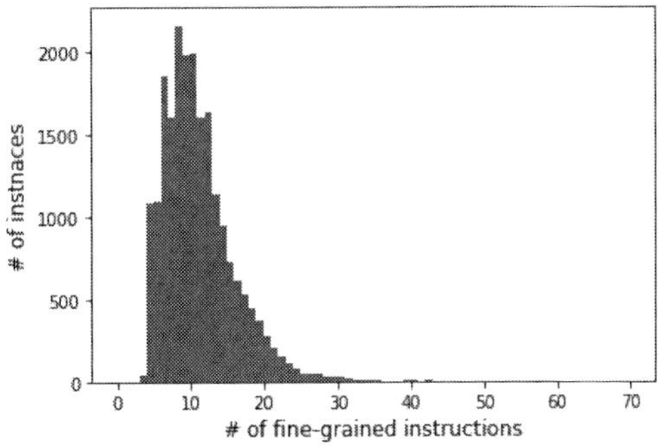

Figure 2: The distribution of the number of fine-grained instructions in the training split

To simplify training and evaluation, we preprocess data by merging the same consecutive actions into one single action. This results in the average sequence length of 25. The entire distribution before and after the merge preprocessing is shown in Figure3 and 4.

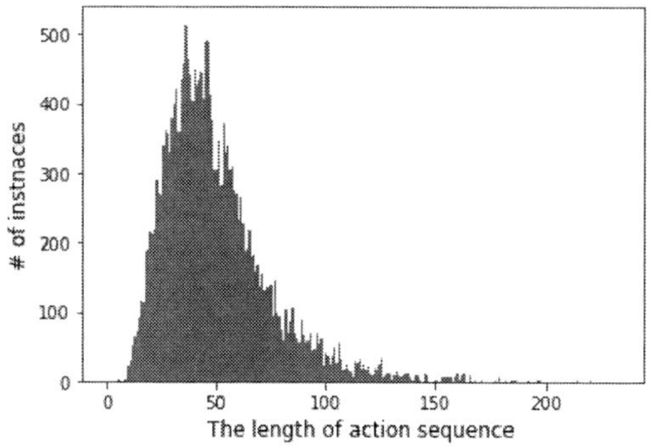

Figure 3: The distribution of action sequence length in the training split.

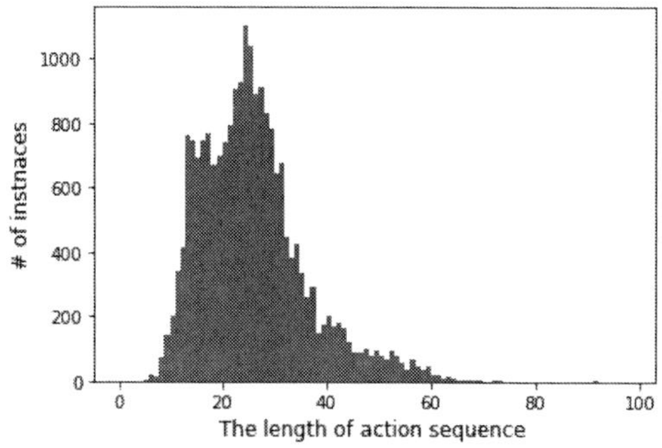

Figure 4: The distribution of action sequence length in the training split after the merge preprocessing.

C Additional Results for the Segmentation Task

Here we compare different strategies for encoding instruction segments. Besides the mean pooling of word embeddings followed by a linear layer in A2LCTC (MEAN), we also tried the summation of word embeddings (SUM), the mean pooling of one-layer Bi-LSTM outputs LSTM. The hidden size of LSTM is set to 50, which is the same as the word embeddings, and the vectors of the forward and backward directions were summed to form the output vectors. The result is shown in Table 6.

	valid_seen		*valid_unseen*	
	EM	F1	EM	F1
MEAN	41.2 ± 10.2	78.2 ± 10.8	44.5 ± 12.1	79.0 ± 11.5
SUM	34.5 ± 13.8	70.7 ± 15.2	36.8 ± 8.4	73.3 ± 12.1
LSTM	18.9 ± 10.8	51.8 ± 20.3	33.8 ± 18.2	65.1 ± 20.6

Table 6: Performance for sub-task segmentation. The value of A2LCTC is the best among 10 runs with different random seeds.

We find that MEAN gives the most stable result. LSTM exhibits the worst performance, indicating that it is hard to optimize the unsupervised objective in A2LCTC with an overly complex architecture.

D Additional Results for the Downstream Task

D.1 Results with the ground-truth sub-goal annotation

In section 4, we compared the models trained with automatically generated fine-grained sub-task segments. Here we provide the results from the model trained with the ground-truth sub-goal segments (SUBGOAL) in Table 7. Note that the granularity of SUBGOAL is coarser than the other models.

	valid_seen	*valid_unseen*
BASELINE	57.6 ± 2.0	29.6 ± 1.5
SUBGOAL	59.5 ± 2.1	31.4 ± 1.4
UNIFORM	63.6 ± 2.5	38.8 ± 1.4
BPE	66.0 ± 2.0	39.1 ± 0.4
A2LCTC	69.7 ± 1.4	41.4 ± 0.8

Table 7: Performance on the ALFRED task measured by the subgoal sequence accuracy. The values show the mean and standard deviation of 5 runs.

SUBGOAL provides better results than BASELINE, which demonstrates the benefit of the ground-truth sub-gold segmentation in the dataset. However, the improvement is limited compared to the UNIFORM segmentation, which segments an action sequence into the chunks of the same size. The model benefits from inaccurate but finer-grained segmentation more than accurate but coarse segmentation.

We hypothesize that this reflects the characteristics of the dataset. The ALFRED dataset is created by generating expert trajectories from task templates. As a result, the type of actions are somewhat correlated with the time step within an episode. For example, navigation actions such as `MoveForward` are more likely to be executed at the beginning of the episode, whereas interactive actions such as `PutObject` are at the end. Adding finer-grained progress monitoring supervision at training time can help the agent learn the correlation between time steps and actions better than coarser progress monitoring.

D.2 Success Rates of the Downstream Task

In our preliminary experiments, we find the original navigation task is too difficult for the baseline model: the success rate is very low with high variance, which prevents meaningful comparison among the variants of the model. The success rate (SC) and goal condition success rate (GC) are provided on Table 8. With multiple runs, we did not observe any significant difference ($p > 0.05$ in the Welch's t-test) among the models.

	SC		GC	
	valid_seen	*valid_unseen*	*valid_seen*	*valid_unseen*
Baseline	2.4 ± 0.9	0.0 ± 0.0	9.5 ± 0.5	6.7 ± 0.3
SUBGOAL	2.6 ± 0.5	0.0 ± 0.0	8.9 ± 0.8	6.6 ± 0.4
A2LCTC	2.3 ± 0.7	0.0 ± 0.0	9.4 ± 0.8	6.7 ± 0.3

Table 8: Performance on the ALFRED task measured by the task success rate (SC) and goal condition success rate (GC). The values show the mean and standard deviation of 5 runs.

GrammarSHAP: An Efficient Model-Agnostic and Structure-Aware NLP Explainer

Edoardo Mosca
TU Munich,
Department of Informatics,
Germany
edoardo.mosca@tum.de

Defne Demitürk
TU Munich,
Department of Informatics,
Germany
ge75yod@mytum.de

Luca Mülln
TU Munich,
Department of Informatics,
Germany
luca.muelln@tum.de

Fabio Raffagnato
TU Munich,
Department of Informatics,
Germany
ga24giv@mytum.de

Georg Groh
TU Munich,
Department of Informatics,
Germany
grohg@in.tum.de

Abstract

Interpreting NLP models is fundamental for their development as it can shed light on hidden properties and unexpected behaviors. However, while transformer architectures exploit contextual information to enhance their predictive capabilities, most of the available methods to explain such predictions only provide importance scores at the word level. This work addresses the lack of feature attribution approaches that also take into account the sentence structure. We extend the SHAP framework by proposing GrammarSHAP—a model-agnostic explainer leveraging the sentence's constituency parsing to generate hierarchical importance scores.

1 Introduction

Deep learning models have raised the bar in terms of performance in a variety of *Natural Language Processing* (NLP) tasks (Vaswani et al., 2017; Devlin et al., 2019). However, also model complexity has been steadily increasing, which in turn hinders the interpretability of their predictions. This is particularly true for transformer architectures, currently established as the state of the art in various applications but at the same time containing billions of parameters (Brown et al., 2020).

Local explanations have become a popular tool to understand and interpret models' decisions (Madsen et al., 2021; Arrieta et al., 2020). These—besides increasing the public's trust in machine learning systems—can uncover unwanted behaviors such as unintended bias (Madsen et al., 2021; Dixon et al., 2018).

Feature attribution explanations are the most commonly used and can highlight parts of the input text that are relevant for the obtained outcome (Lundberg and Lee, 2017; Ribeiro et al., 2016). Almost all available methods, however, can only attribute a relevance score to single words. This is highly unintuitive as natural language in human communication can be very articulated and context-dependent. Indeed, a word's neighborhood can drastically alter its intended message and sentiment.

Our work focuses on generating explanations that account for the language structure. More specifically, we build hierarchical explanations that attribute relevance scores to sentence constituents at multiple levels. In contrast to previous work addressing the same issue (Chen et al., 2020; Chen and Jordan, 2020), we build our approach as an extension of SHAP (Lundberg and Lee, 2017)—a local explainability framework renowned for its solid theoretical background. Our contribution can be summarized as follows:

(1) We design GrammarSHAP, a model-agnostic approach for generating multi-level explanations that consider the text's structure and its constituents. More specifically, a constituency parsing layer for multi-word tokens selection is added before an adapted KernelSHAP explainer.

(2) We propose to drop the SHAP standard background dataset and use masking tokens instead. This reduces unwanted artifacts in the generated explanations and speeds up the approach's run time.

Proceedings of the First Workshop on Learning with Natural Language Supervision, pages 10 - 16
May 26, 2022 ©2022 Association for Computational Linguistics

(3) We qualitatively compare our method to existing ones in terms of explanation quality and necessary computational effort.

2 Related Work

Several local explainability techniques exist to interpret predictions produced by NLP models (Arrieta et al., 2020). Among them, *features attribution* (or *feature relevance*) approaches quantify each input component's contribution to the model's output, i.e. how each feature affects the observed prediction. Methods in this category are available in a large variety: gradient-based (Simonyan et al., 2014; Sundararajan et al., 2017), neural-network specific e.g. LRP (Bach et al., 2015) and DeepLIFT (Shrikumar et al., 2017), and model-agnostic e.g. LIME (Ribeiro et al., 2016). SHAP (Lundberg and Lee, 2017)—particularly relevant for our methodology—is by many considered to be a gold standard thanks to its solid theoretical background and broad applicability. This framework builds a unified view of methods like LIME, LRP, and DeepLIFT and the game-theoretic concept of Shapley values (Shapley, 1953).

More recent works address the limitations of word-level relevance scores by focusing on phrase-level and hierarchical explanations. The proposed approaches analyze and quantify words' interactions through exhaustive search (Tsang et al., 2018), combining their contextual decomposition scores (Singh et al., 2018), or via measuring SHAP interaction values along a predefined tree structure (Lundberg et al., 2018). Chen and Jordan (2020) combines a linguistic parse tree with Banzhaf values (Banzhaf III, 1964) to capture meaningful interactions in text inputs. (Chen et al., 2020), instead, propose to detect directly feature interaction without resorting to external structures. They propose a hierarchical explainability method that, in a top-down fashion, breaks down text components in shorter phrases and words based on the weakest detected interactions.

3 Methodology

We extend the SHAP framework (Lundberg and Lee, 2017) by proposing a model-agnostic explainer that considers the text's structural dependencies to generate importance scores at multiple levels. In particular, we couple a constituency parsing layer to hierarchically select multi-word tokens with a custom version of KernelSHAP adapted for improved efficiency and run-time. Figure 1 presents an overview of the methodological pipeline proposed in this work.

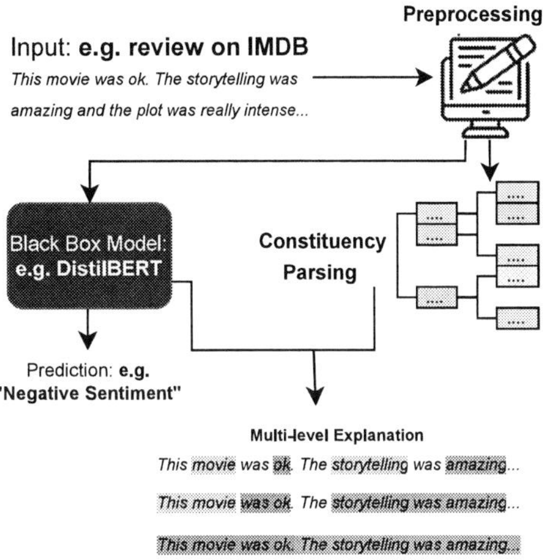

Figure 1: Overview of the proposed methodology.

3.1 Token Selection via Constituency Parsing

To hierarchically construct multi-word tokens in a way that reflects the sentence structure, we leverage constituency parsing to group together tokens based on their grammatical interactions. To this end, we choose a state-of-the-art constituency parser: the Berkeley Neural Parser (Kitaev and Klein, 2018).

We iterate over parsed sentences from the single-word level ($depth = 0$) until the complete sentences are grouped up as a single token ($depth = N$). Additionally, we provide a library to retrieve groups of words at any depth, constituents, and combinations thereof. Our implementation also handles inconsistencies between the word-tokenization of the constituency parser and BERT. This is necessary as BERT's tokenizer uses sub-word tokens to represent OOV words and the Berkley Neural Parser[1] only allows full words as input.

3.2 Efficient Multi-Token Explainer

Our GrammarSHAP explainer directly extends the KernelSHAP method from Lundberg and Lee (2017). As parsed sentences already provide a hierarchical structure of grammatically coherent tokens, our extension is not required to compute tokens interaction to construct importance scores for multi-word tokens.

[1] spacy.io/universe/project/self-attentive-parser

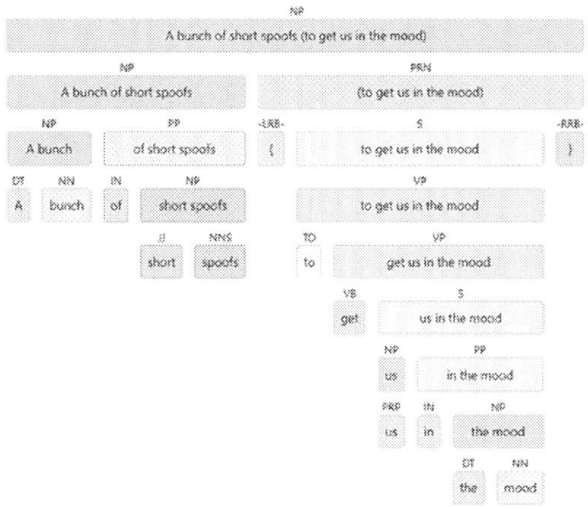

Figure 2: Example of sentence parsed with the Berkeley Neural Parser (Kitaev and Klein, 2018). Tokens are hierarchically grouped from single words (bottom level) to the whole sentence (top level)

KernelSHAP takes an input sample x, a predicting model f, and a background set of samples to be used when replacing tokens to compute feature importance. Tokens belonging to the background dataset are fed to the explainer during initialization. At explanation time, a linear system of all perturbed sentences and their corresponding model predictions is solved to determine the effect of each single feature.

The extension to multi-word tokens consists in feeding the explainer—i.e. KernelSHAP—with the indices corresponding to the features to be grouped. In the case of constituency parsed sentences, indices representing multi-token groups are always adjacent in the input sentence. However, this is not a strict requirement for the following steps of our extension. To obtain group-level feature importance, we constrain the extended explainer to always replace a complete group of words with elements of the background dataset. Analogous to KernelSHAP, the expected effect of each feature group—i.e. its (multi-token) SHAP value—is calculated by solving the linear system of all perturbed sentences with their corresponding outcomes. In summary, our extension behaves like KernelSHAP but treats groups of tokens as single features.

While the calculation of SHAP values on multi-words tokens is a straightforward extension, it leads to several issues:

- **Computationally Expensive:** Computing importance scores for multiple levels further slows down the already inefficient KernelSHAP.
- **Unidirectional:** The explainer only highlights groups with the same sentiment as the overall sentence.
- **High Attribution for [SEP]:** The separation token changes the sentence length when used as replacement from the background data. This causes it to have high relevance for the classifier.

We address these limitation by replacing the background data with **[MASK]** tokens. This leads to a 60-folds speed up of the explainer that is not required to iterate over the background data. Moreover, **[SEP]** does causes explanation artifacts as it is excluded from the background data.

4 Empirical Findings

4.1 Data and Model to be Explained

To test and compare our method in practice, we pick a DistilBERT model (Sanh et al., 2019). Our choice is motivated by transformer architectures being established as the current state of the art in a variety of NLP applications.

Concerning the data, we pick the IMDb movie reviews (Maas et al., 2011) and the SST-2 datasets (Socher et al., 2013). For both, the *Hugging Face*[2] library provides a version of DistilBERT pre-trained on the task of binary sentiment analysis. The accuracy achieved is 93.7% and 91.3% respectively.

4.2 Existing SHAP Baselines

We compare explanations generated with GrammarSHAP with two existing baselines from the SHAP framework (Lundberg and Lee, 2017):

(1) PartitionSHAP, i.e. the library's current recommended method for sentiment analisys on text data. Similarly to our method, it also utilizes **[MASK]** tokens for efficient word removal. However, features are only grouped via a binary tree and thus only token pairs are considered at a given hierarchical level.

(2) KernelSHAP, i.e. the library's standard for model-agnostic explanations. KernelSHAP only produces word-level explanations by default. But thanks to the additive nature of Shapley values,

[2] https://huggingface.co/textattack/distilbert-base-uncased-imdb

these can be added together according to the constituency parsing tree. We will refer to this custom hierarchical version of KernelSHAP as *Additive KernelSHAP*.

4.3 Comparison

The three methods substantially differ both in terms of generation times and explanation quality. Table 1 reports the average running time to produce an explanation. Figures 3 and 4 show—starting from the same input text—the explanations generated with each method. The text sample is particularly instructive as it contains both positive- and negative-sentiment sentences.

Method	Running Time
PartitionSHAP	2
Add. KernelSHAP	3554 (~1h)
GrammarSHAP	183 (~3min)

Table 1: Average running time (in seconds) for GrammarSHAP compared to the existing SHAP baselines. The running time has been measured on 20 randomly selected samples (10 from IMDb and 10 from SST-2). Results were measured on a laptop machine: AMD Ryzen 5 CPU, Nvidia GPU GeForce GTX 1650, 16 GB DDR4 RAM.

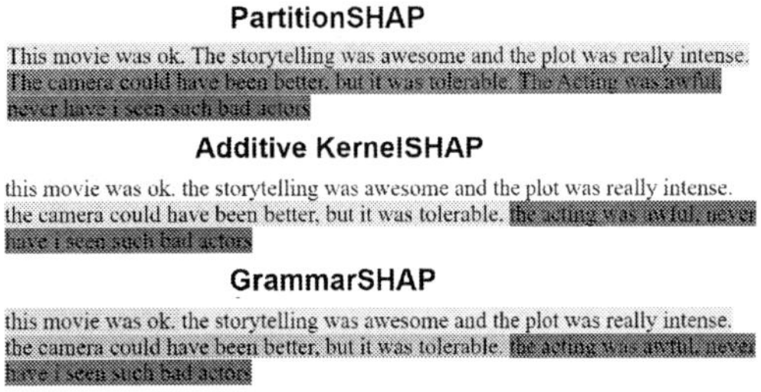

Figure 3: Comparison of three explanation methods for grouped features relevance (5th level). DistilBERT predicted the sample's sentiment as negative with a 79.5% confidence.

Figure 4: Comparison of three explanation methods for grouped features relevance (5th level). DistilBERT predicted the sample's sentiment as negative with a 81.8% confidence.

PartitionSHAP is very efficient and the fastest method among the compared ones. However, it is quite coarse in grouping together tokens and fails to identify fine-grained contributions at the sub-sentence level. Additive KernelSHAP has an extremely long execution time and is the slowest of the three approaches. Moreover, it does not identify contributions opposite to the sample's overall sentiment. In contrast, GrammarSHAP is able to identify both negative and positive sentiments at different (hierarchical) levels of granularity. In terms of efficiency, GrammarSHAP does not match the performance of PartitionSHAP. However, its running time is still reasonable and does not raise issues for most applications.

More examples of hierarchical GrammarSHAP explanation on (long) texts are provided in the appendix (see A). There, we also focus on presenting the explanations at different levels of granularity.

5 Limitations and Future Work

GrammarSHAP meaningfully extends the SHAP framework by providing efficient hierarchical explanations that reflect the sentence structure. However, limitations of our methodology and experimentation need to be acknowledged and motivate our future work.

Regarding the explanation quality, our evaluation process is based on the introduced methodological improvements and on a qualitative analysis of the produced explanations. Although evaluation metrics for explanations are complex to define and have not been standardized yet, our comparison would considerably benefit from the usage of quantitative diagnostic properties (Atanasova et al., 2020) and word-level level metrics (Nguyen, 2018; Samek et al., 2016).

In terms of execution time, our method is still reasonable considering the granularity of contributions that it can detect. However, the necessity for further improvements in terms of efficiency becomes apparent when producing real-time explanations on the large scale.

6 Conclusion

In this work we proposed GrammarSHAP: a model-agnostic explainer for text data that accounts for the sentence structure and the existing grammatical relationships between the text tokens. Our approach leverages constituency parsing to extend the SHAP framework by providing hierarchical explanations that go beyond word-level attribution scores.

Our qualitative analysis of the produced explanation yields promising results as GrammarSHAP appears to identify more fine-grained contribution in structured text than its existing SHAP counterparts. At the same time, the usage of masking tokens instead of a background dataset considerably speeds up its execution in comparison with KernalSHAP. These properties make GrammarSHAP also suitable for long texts, especially if they contain sentences carrying different types of sentiment. As a first priority for our future work, we will focus on the quantitative evaluation the produced explanation.

References

Alejandro Barredo Arrieta, Natalia Díaz-Rodríguez, Javier Del Ser, Adrien Bennetot, Siham Tabik, Alberto Barbado, Salvador García, Sergio Gil-López, Daniel Molina, Richard Benjamins, et al. 2020. Explainable artificial intelligence (xai): Concepts, taxonomies, opportunities and challenges toward responsible ai. *Information Fusion*, 58:82–115.

Pepa Atanasova, Jakob Grue Simonsen, Christina Lioma, and Isabelle Augenstein. 2020. A diagnostic study of explainability techniques for text classification. In *Proceedings of the 2020 Conference on Empirical Methods in Natural Language Processing (EMNLP)*, pages 3256–3274.

Sebastian Bach, Alexander Binder, Grégoire Montavon, Frederick Klauschen, Klaus-Robert Müller, and Wojciech Samek. 2015. On pixel-wise explanations for non-linear classifier decisions by layer-wise relevance propagation. *PloS one*, 10(7):130–140.

John F Banzhaf III. 1964. Weighted voting doesn't work: A mathematical analysis. *Rutgers L. Rev.*, 19:317.

Tom Brown, Benjamin Mann, Nick Ryder, Melanie Subbiah, Jared D Kaplan, Prafulla Dhariwal, Arvind Neelakantan, Pranav Shyam, Girish Sastry, Amanda Askell, Sandhini Agarwal, Ariel Herbert-Voss, Gretchen Krueger, Tom Henighan, Rewon Child, Aditya Ramesh, Daniel Ziegler, Jeffrey Wu, Clemens Winter, Chris Hesse, Mark Chen, Eric Sigler, Mateusz Litwin, Scott Gray, Benjamin Chess, Jack Clark, Christopher Berner, Sam McCandlish, Alec Radford, Ilya Sutskever, and Dario Amodei. 2020. Language models are few-shot learners. In *Advances in Neural Information Processing Systems*, volume 33, pages 1877–1901. Curran Associates, Inc.

Hanjie Chen, Guangtao Zheng, and Yangfeng Ji. 2020. Generating hierarchical explanations on text classification via feature interaction detection. In *Proceedings of the 58th Annual Meeting of the Association for Computational Linguistics*, pages 5578–5593.

Jianbo Chen and Michael Jordan. 2020. Ls-tree: Model interpretation when the data are linguistic. In *Proceedings of the AAAI Conference on Artificial Intelligence*, volume 34, pages 3454–3461.

Jacob Devlin, Ming-Wei Chang, Kenton Lee, and Kristina Toutanova. 2019. Bert: Pre-training of deep bidirectional transformers for language understanding. In *NAACL-HLT (1)*.

Lucas Dixon, John Li, Jeffrey Sorensen, Nithum Thain, and Lucy Vasserman. 2018. Measuring and mitigating unintended bias in text classification. In *Proceedings of the 2018 AAAI/ACM Conference on AI, Ethics, and Society*, pages 67–73.

Nikita Kitaev and Dan Klein. 2018. Constituency parsing with a self-attentive encoder. In *Proceedings of the 56th Annual Meeting of the Association for Computational Linguistics (Volume 1: Long Papers)*, pages 2676–2686, Melbourne, Australia. Association for Computational Linguistics.

Scott M Lundberg, Gabriel G Erion, and Su-In Lee. 2018. Consistent individualized feature attribution for tree ensembles. *arXiv preprint arXiv:1802.03888*.

Scott M. Lundberg and Su-In Lee. 2017. A unified approach to interpreting model predictions. *NeurIPS 2017*.

Andrew L. Maas, Raymond E. Daly, Peter T. Pham, Dan Huang, Andrew Y. Ng, and Christopher Potts. 2011. Learning word vectors for sentiment analysis. In *Proceedings of the 49th Annual Meeting of the Association for Computational Linguistics: Human Language Technologies*, pages 142–150, Portland, Oregon, USA. Association for Computational Linguistics.

Andreas Madsen, Siva Reddy, and Sarath Chandar. 2021. Post-hoc interpretability for neural nlp: A survey. *arXiv preprint arXiv:2108.04840*.

Dong Nguyen. 2018. Comparing automatic and human evaluation of local explanations for text classification. In *Proceedings of the 2018 Conference of the North American Chapter of the Association for Computational Linguistics: Human Language Technologies, Volume 1 (Long Papers)*, pages 1069–1078.

Marco Tulio Ribeiro, Sameer Singh, and Carlos Guestrin. 2016. " why should i trust you?" explaining the predictions of any classifier. In *Proceedings of the 22nd ACM SIGKDD international conference on knowledge discovery and data mining*, pages 1135–1144.

Wojciech Samek, Alexander Binder, Grégoire Montavon, Sebastian Lapuschkin, and Klaus-Robert Müller. 2016. Evaluating the visualization of what a deep neural network has learned. *IEEE transactions on neural networks and learning systems*, 28(11):2660–2673.

Victor Sanh, Lysandre Debut, Julien Chaumond, and Thomas Wolf. 2019. Distilbert, a distilled version of bert: smaller, faster, cheaper and lighter. *NeurIPS 2017*.

Lloyd S Shapley. 1953. A value for n-person games. *Contributions to the Theory of Games 2.28*, page 307–317.

Avanti Shrikumar, Peyton Greenside, and Anshul Kundaje. 2017. Learning important features through propagating activation differences. In *Proceedings of the 34th International Conference on Machine Learning-Volume 70*, pages 3145–3153.

Karen Simonyan, Andrea Vedaldi, and Andrew Zisserman. 2014. Deep inside convolutional networks: Visualising image classification models and saliency maps. In *2nd International Conference on Learning Representations, ICLR 2014*.

Chandan Singh, W James Murdoch, and Bin Yu. 2018. Hierarchical interpretations for neural network predictions. In *International Conference on Learning Representations*.

Richard Socher, Alex Perelygin, Jean Wu, Jason Chuang, Christopher D. Manning, Andrew Ng, and Christopher Potts. 2013. Recursive deep models for semantic compositionality over a sentiment treebank. In *Proceedings of the 2013 Conference on Empirical Methods in Natural Language Processing*, pages 1631–1642, Seattle, Washington, USA. Association for Computational Linguistics.

Mukund Sundararajan, Ankur Taly, and Qiqi Yan. 2017. Axiomatic attribution for deep networks. In *Proceedings of the 34th International Conference on Machine Learning-Volume 70*, pages 3319–3328. JMLR. org.

Michael Tsang, Youbang Sun, Dongxu Ren, and Yan Liu. 2018. Can i trust you more? model-agnostic hierarchical explanations. *arXiv preprint arXiv:1812.04801*.

Ashish Vaswani, Noam Shazeer, Niki Parmar, Jakob Uszkoreit, Llion Jones, Aidan N. Gomez, Lukasz Kaiser, and Illia Polosukhin. 2017. Attention is all you need. *NIPS 2017*.

A Explanations Examples

Figure 5 shows an example of hierarchical GrammarSHAP explanation on a long text while 6 rather focuses on a shorter text. More examples can be found in the code repository attached to our submission. These are in the *Graphics Interchange Format* (GIF) format to visualize the transformation of the relevance scores through the various hierarchical levels.

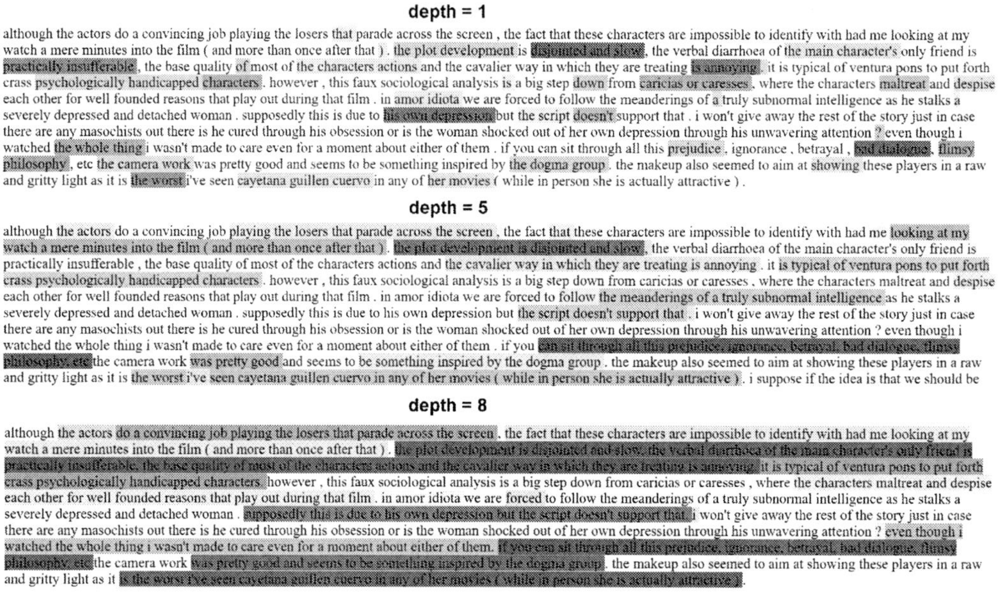

Figure 5: Explanation generated with GrammarSHAP on a long IMDB review with negative-sentiment prediction of 91.7%. From top to bottom, relevance scores at the 1st, 5th and 8th hierarchical level.

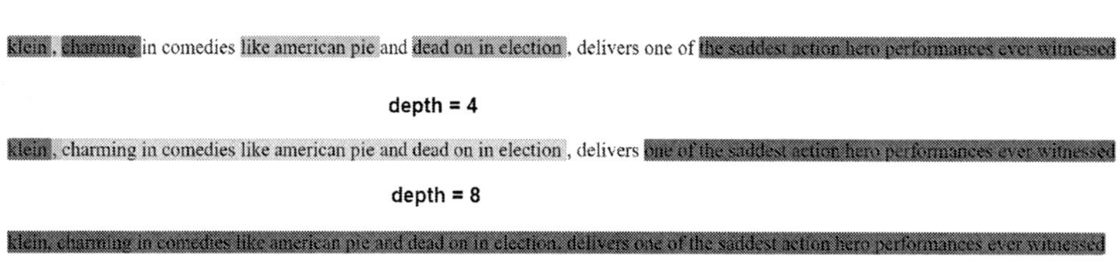

Figure 6: Explanation generated with GrammarSHAP on a short SST-2 review with negative-sentiment prediction of 91.6%. From top to bottom, relevance scores at the 2nd, 4th and 8th hierarchical level.

Single-Turn Debate Does Not Help Humans Answer Hard Reading-Comprehension Questions

Alicia Parrish,[1]* Harsh Trivedi,[2]* Ethan Perez,[1]* Angelica Chen,[1] Nikita Nangia,[1] Jason Phang,[1] Samuel R. Bowman[1]

[1]New York University [2]Stony Brook University

Correspondence: alicia.v.parrish@nyu.edu, bowman@nyu.edu

Abstract

Current QA systems can generate reasonable-sounding yet false answers without explanation or evidence for the generated answer, which is especially problematic when humans cannot readily check the model's answers. This presents a challenge for building trust in machine learning systems. We take inspiration from real-world situations where difficult questions are answered by considering opposing sides (see Irving et al., 2018). For multiple-choice QA examples, we build a dataset of single arguments for both a correct and incorrect answer option in a debate-style set-up as an initial step in training models to produce *explanations* for two candidate answers. We use long contexts—humans familiar with the context write convincing explanations for pre-selected correct and incorrect answers, and we test if those explanations allow humans *who have not read the full context* to more accurately determine the correct answer. We do not find that explanations in our set-up improve human accuracy, but a baseline condition shows that providing human-selected text snippets does improve accuracy. We use these findings to suggest ways of improving the debate set up for future data collection efforts.

1 Introduction

Challenging questions that humans cannot easily determine a correct answer for (e.g., in political debates or courtrooms) often require people to consider opposing viewpoints and weigh multiple pieces of evidence to determine the most appropriate answer. We take inspiration from this to explore whether debate-style explanations can improve how reliably humans can use NLP or question answering (QA) systems to answer questions they cannot readily determine the ground-truth answer for.

As QA models improve, we have the opportunity to use them to aid humans, but current models do not reliably provide correct answers and, instead, often provide believable yet false responses (Nakano et al., 2021, i.a.). Without access to the ground truth, humans cannot directly determine if an answer is false, especially if that answer comes with a convincing-sounding explanation. A solution could be for QA systems to generate explanations with evidence alongside different answer options, allowing humans to serve as judges and assess the validity of the model's competing explanations (Irving et al., 2018). This approach may be most useful when humans cannot readily determine the ground truth. This is the case for dense technical text requiring expert knowledge and for long texts where the answer is retrievable, but it would take significant time; we consider the latter as a case study.

We create a dataset of answer explanations to long-context multiple choice questions from QuALITY (Pang et al., 2021) as an initial step in this direction. The explanations are arguments for predetermined answer options; crucially, we collect explanations for both a correct and incorrect option, each with supporting evidence from the passage, to create debate-style explanations. To assess the viability of this data format, we test if humans can more accurately determine the correct answer when provided with debate-style explanations.

We find that the explanations do not improve human accuracy compared to baseline conditions without those explanations. This negative result may be specific to the chosen task set-up, so we report the results and release the current dataset as a tool for future research on generating and evaluating QA explanations. We offer concrete suggestions for future work that builds on the current dataset and alters the task set up in a way that allows humans to more accurately determine the correct answer. The ultimate goal is to develop a fine-tuning dataset for models that can both explain why a potential answer option is correct and cite

* Equal contribution.

Proceedings of the First Workshop on Learning with Natural Language Supervision, pages 17 - 28

the evidence that is the basis for that explanation in a way that humans find understandable and helpful, *even in the context of an unreliable system.*

2 Related Work

Prior work has explored using models to generate explanations (Camburu et al., 2018; Rajani et al., 2019; Zellers et al., 2019), but there is limited work on using those explanations to verify the model's prediction, particularly when a human cannot perform the task directly. Such a dataset would be useful, as model explanations can aid humans in tasks such as medical diagnosis (Cai et al., 2019; Lundberg et al., 2018), data annotation (Schmidt and Biessmann, 2019) and deception detection (Lai and Tan, 2019). However, Bansal et al. (2021) highlight that these studies use models that outperform humans at the task in question, undermining the motivation for providing a model's explanation alongside its prediction. When the performance of models and humans is similar, current explanation methods do not significantly help humans perform tasks more accurately (Bansal et al., 2021). However, explanations based on a mental model of the human's predicted actions and goals can reduce task completion time (Gao et al., 2020). We address these shortcomings by collecting data for training models to provide explanations on tasks that would otherwise be time-consuming for humans.

In addition to task characteristics, several qualities of the model explanation affect the helpfulness of human-AI collaboration: Machine-generated explanations only improve human performance when the explanations are not too complex (Ai et al., 2021; Narayanan et al., 2018). And though users want explanations of how models mark answers incorrect, most explanations that models output focus on the option selected (Liao et al., 2020). Our dataset addresses this by including evidence and explanations for both correct and incorrect options to each question, enabling models trained on it to present arguments for more than one answer.

3 Argument Writing Protocol

We build a dataset of QA (counter-)explanations by having human writers read a long passage and construct arguments with supporting evidence for one of two answer options. We then present the explanations side-by-side to a human judge working under a strict time constraint, who selects which answer is correct given the two explanations.

Passage and Question Selection We use passages and questions from a draft version of the recent long-document QA dataset, QuALITY (Pang et al., 2021). In QuALITY, most passages are science fiction stories of about 5k words with 20 four-option multiple-choice questions. We determine which of the three incorrect options is best suited to have a convincing argument by identifying cases where (i) humans in a time-limited setting incorrectly selected that choice at least 3/5 times, and/or (ii) humans who read the entire passage selected that choice as the best distractor item more than half the time. We discard questions without an incorrect answer option meeting either criteria.

Writing Task We recruit 14 experienced writers via the freelancing platform Upwork (writer selection details are in Appendix A). We assign each writer up to 26 passages. Each passage has 7–15 2-option multiple choice questions (avg. of 13.3). We have writers construct an argument (max 500 characters) and select 1–3 supporting text snippets (max 250 characters) for one of those two options (Table 1), with the rate of correct and incorrect options assigned to each writer roughly equal.

We encourage writing effective arguments by awarding writers a bonus each time a worker in the judging task selects the answer they wrote an argument for. Including bonuses, workers average $21.04/hr, after taking Upwork fees into account. Further details are in Appendix A, and a description of the writing interface is in Appendix B.

Final Dataset We release a dataset of both correct and incorrect arguments with selected text snippets and the results of the judgment experiment as a tool for researchers. These datasets are available at github.com/nyu-mll/single_turn_debate. As we use passages from a draft version of QuALITY, we do not release arguments from passages in their non-public test set. The final dataset that we release contains 2944 arguments (50% correct) from 112 unique passages, each with an average of 2.4 text snippets.

4 Judging Protocol

We test the effectiveness of the arguments by having human judges answer the multiple-choice question. To ensure that the judges cannot simply read the passage to find the answer themselves, we give them only 90 seconds of access to the passage along with the arguments and text snippets. To determine

Question: *What clearly showed a sense humbleness presented by Si?*			
Correct option: *His lack of awareness that he would be considered a celebrity at the Kudos Room.*		**Incorrect option**: *His quaint behavior at the banquet where he was presented with a gold watch.*	
Argument	**Text snippets**	**Argument**	**Text Snippets**
Si clearly puts the Kudos Room on a pedestal as a place for the top echelons of society and feels humbled to be sitting there, even thinking back to how he dreamed about it while sitting in his space craft (#1). He seems taken aback when Natalie recognises him as the famous space pilot and even seems to downplay his status and accomplishments (#2). While Natalie seems star-struck by his presence, he seems equally star-stuck by her beauty, showing how humble he is despite being famous (#3).	(1) Well, this was something like it. This was the sort of thing he'd dreamed about, out there in the great alone, seated in the confining conning tower of his space craft. He sipped at the drink, finding it up to his highest expectations (2) The girl, her voice suddenly subtly changed, said, "Why, isn't that a space pin?" Si, disconcerted by the sudden reversal, said, "Yeah ... sure." (3) Imagine meeting Seymour Pond. Just sitting down next to him at a bar. Just like that. "Si," Si said, gratified. Holy Zoroaster, he'd never seen anything like this rarified pulchritude. Maybe on teevee	It's clear from #1 and #2 that in the professional world in which Si moved, a high standard of living was expected. Symbols of prestige were also considered desirable in this social world, reflected by him being awarded a gold watch (see #3). However, it's clear that Si doesn't care for symbols of prestige like gold watches, prefer more practical items instead Nor is he desirous of a higher standard of living. He only wants enough money to meet life's necessities.	(1) They hadn't figured he had enough shares of Basic to see him through decently. Well, possibly he didn't, given their standards. But Space Pilot Seymour Pond didn't have their standards. (2) He'd had plenty of time to think it over. It was better to retire on a limited crediting, on a confoundedly limited crediting, than to take the two or three more trips in hopes of attaining a higher standard. (3) In common with recipients of gold watches of a score of generations before him, Si Pond would have preferred something a bit more tangible in the way of reward

Table 1: Example of opposing arguments, with extracted evidence, for two options to a question from QuALITY about a science-fiction story. The full passage for this example is at gutenberg.org/ebooks/52995.

whether the arguments affect human accuracy, we compare the performance of workers who see those arguments and snippets to the performance of workers who do not see the arguments and workers who see neither the arguments nor the text snippets.

Judging Task Protocol We recruit 194 workers via Amazon Mechanical Turk (MTurk; recruitment details are in Appendix C). Each worker judges which of two answer options is correct, given just 90 seconds. The worker has unlimited time to read the question and answer options before starting a 90-second timer. Once the timer is started, the worker can view the entire passage, as well as the arguments and text snippets for each answer option. Clicking on the snippets scrolls to and highlights the relevant section of the passage so that the snippet can be viewed in context. Once the timer runs out, the worker has 30 seconds to finalize their answer before the task auto-submits, though workers can submit their answer at any time. After submitting, workers see immediate feedback about their accuracy to help them improve over time and to increase engagement. Each question is judged by three unique workers, and we ensure workers are paying attention with catch trials (Appendix E). Details on the judging interface are in Appendix D.

Payment and Bonus Structure Workers receive $0.15 per task and a bonus of $0.40 for each correct answer. We aim for the low base pay and generous bonuses to disincentivize guessing. Assuming workers spend 90 seconds per task, including reading the question and answer options,[2] a worker with an accuracy of 65% earns $16.40/hr.

Baselines We include two additional conditions to better understand the effects of arguments in this time-limited setting. The main protocol is the **passage+snippet+argument condition (PSA)**. The baselines present just the **passage+snippet (PS)** or just the **passage with no supporting evidence (P)**. All other details of the protocol remain the same. Each worker only sees tasks in one condition at a time, but through three rounds of data collection, they alternate through the conditions in a random and counterbalanced way. No worker judges the same question in multiple conditions.

Pilot Judges During the writing phase, we use a smaller pool of workers who we qualify as an initial group of judges to gather feedback for the writers and determine their bonuses. In this group, five judges rate each question, and we test the effects of different time limits, which vary in different rounds between 60, 90, or 120 seconds. These pilot results are not part of our main results, but we include the pilot results and details about the pilot judges in

[2]Median completion times after starting the timer were about 60s, so total completion times were likely <90s.

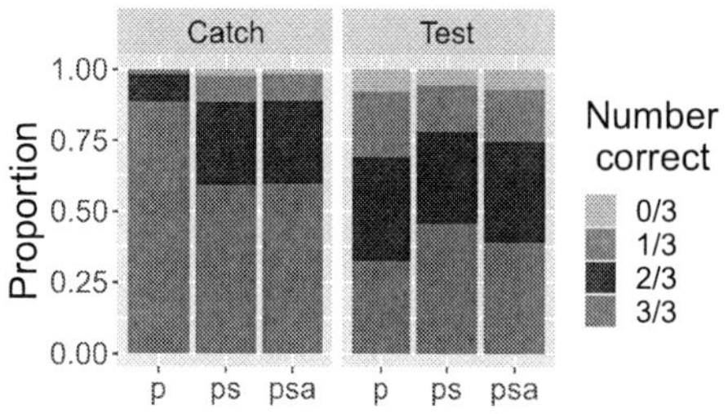

Figure 1: Proportion of workers who answered each question correctly in each condition. P is passage; S is snippets; A is arguments

Appendix F. All other task details are the same as for the main judges.

5 Results

In addition to the primary comparison across conditions, we conduct exploratory analyses to better understand effects of the task set-up on workers' response behavior. Results on features of arguments and text snippets are in Appendix I.

Comparison Across Conditions Workers are more accurate when they have access to text snippets, and they are the most accurate in the PS condition, indicating no clear effect of the arguments. Figure 1 shows the accuracy rates by question in each of the conditions. Both unanimous agreement (3/3 workers correct) and majority vote agreement ($\geq$2/3 workers correct) show that workers are most accurate in PS and least accurate in P.

Effects of Time We investigate if workers get more accurate at this task over time to see if they are learning task-specific strategies. Workers' accuracy does improve slightly over time, by about 4 percentage points in each condition between the first 10 tasks and final 10 (Appendix I, Figure 8). The accuracy increase is small and could be accounted for by workers becoming more familiar with the task format or by figuring out a moderately effective strategy.

Most workers submit an answer before the 90s timer ends. Median completion times are longest in P (69s) and similar between PS (54s) and PSA (57s). The average time spent varies by worker, so we check if spending more time leads to higher accuracy. However, there is no correlation between workers' average task time and average accuracy (Appendix I, Figure 9).

Follow-up Survey We release a paid survey to workers who completed at least 10 tasks in each condition to ask about what strategies they used and to better understand their reactions to the arguments. 102 workers qualified for the survey, and 91 completed it. Workers who reported reading the snippets had significantly higher accuracy in PS and PSA compared to workers who did not report reading them. However, there are no significant differences in PSA accuracy based on whether the workers reported reading the arguments or ignoring them. A quarter of workers reported mistrusting the arguments; though mistrust does not correlate with performance, see Appendix I for discussion.

6 Discussion

We find it likely that explanations will be beneficial to users in *some* tasks under *some* conditions. The prevalence of a debate-style set up in real-world settings (e.g., courtrooms[3]) makes this an *a priori* reasonable area for systematic exploration, but the current study is limited in its scope and is not strong evidence against the broad potential usefulness of such a set-up. The current experiments are a case study in creating a scenario where humans are *unable* to be sure about their answer, but they have access to evidence to help identify the correct response. The finding that a quarter of workers mistrusted the arguments raises the issue of whether an approach that gives users misleading information from the outset is on the wrong track. However, we already know QA models provide false and misleading information; this behavior has the potential to be *more* harmful when it is not explicit that generated explanations may be wrong.

One reason that the arguments were more misleading than helpful to some workers could be that the correct and incorrect arguments were *independent* of each other. The strength of debate for determining the true answer could rely on counter-arguments that explicitly reference deficiencies of the other argument. It is therefore possible that a *multi-turn* setting is needed for debate to be helpful, but we leave this as a question for future research.

The time limit that we use makes the task more artificial than we'd like. However, pilot results (Appendix F) show that variations between 60 and 120 seconds make virtually no difference in performance. It is possible that 120s is still too short, and so workers rushed through the task as much as they

[3]We are *not* suggesting this be used in *actual* courtrooms.

did with 60s, but we would have expected this to vary more by worker, and the general trend is that people are slightly *less* accurate at 120s than at 90s.

7 Conclusion

We set out to test whether providing users with arguments for opposing answer options in a multiple choice QA task could help humans be more accurate, even when they haven't read the passage. The results indicate that the task set up had little to no effect on accuracy, but it raises new questions and possible future directions for when such explanations may be useful.

Acknowledgements

This project has benefited from financial support to SB by Eric and Wendy Schmidt (made by recommendation of the Schmidt Futures program), Samsung Research (under the project *Improving Deep Learning using Latent Structure*) and Apple. This material is based upon work supported by the National Science Foundation under Grant Nos. 1922658 and 2046556. Any opinions, findings, and conclusions or recommendations expressed in this material are those of the authors and do not necessarily reflect the views of the National Science Foundation.

References

Lun Ai, Stephen H Muggleton, Céline Hocquette, Mark Gromowski, and Ute Schmid. 2021. Beneficial and harmful explanatory machine learning. *Machine Learning*, 110(4):695–721.

Gagan Bansal, Tongshuang Wu, Joyce Zhou, Raymond Fok, Besmira Nushi, Ece Kamar, Marco Tulio Ribeiro, and Daniel Weld. 2021. Does the whole exceed its parts? the effect of ai explanations on complementary team performance. CHI '21, New York, NY, USA. Association for Computing Machinery.

Carrie J. Cai, Samantha Winter, David Steiner, Lauren Wilcox, and Michael Terry. 2019. "Hello AI": Uncovering the onboarding needs of medical practitioners for human-AI collaborative decision-making. *Proc. ACM Hum.-Comput. Interact.*, 3(CSCW).

Oana-Maria Camburu, Tim Rocktäschel, Thomas Lukasiewicz, and Phil Blunsom. 2018. e-SNLI: Natural language inference with natural language explanations. In *Advances in Neural Information Processing Systems*, volume 31. Curran Associates, Inc.

Xiaofeng Gao, Ran Gong, Yizhou Zhao, Shu Wang, Tianmin Shu, and Song-Chun Zhu. 2020. Joint mind modeling for explanation generation in complex human-robot collaborative tasks. In *2020 29th IEEE International Conference on Robot and Human Interactive Communication (RO-MAN)*, pages 1119–1126.

Geoffrey Irving, Paul Christiano, and Dario Amodei. 2018. AI safety via debate. *arXiv preprint arXiv:1805.00899*.

Vivian Lai and Chenhao Tan. 2019. On human predictions with explanations and predictions of machine learning models: A case study on deception detection. In *Proceedings of the Conference on Fairness, Accountability, and Transparency*, FAT* '19, page 29–38, New York, NY, USA. Association for Computing Machinery.

Q. Vera Liao, Daniel Gruen, and Sarah Miller. 2020. *Questioning the AI: Informing Design Practices for Explainable AI User Experiences*, page 1–15. Association for Computing Machinery, New York, NY, USA.

Scott M. Lundberg, B. Nair, M. Vavilala, M. Horibe, M. Eisses, Trevor Adams, D. Liston, Daniel King-Wai Low, Shu-Fang Newman, J. Kim, and Su-In Lee. 2018. Explainable machine-learning predictions for the prevention of hypoxaemia during surgery. *Nature biomedical engineering*, 2:749 – 760.

Reiichiro Nakano, Jacob Hilton, Suchir Balaji, Jeff Wu, Long Ouyang, Christina Kim, Christopher Hesse, Shantanu Jain, Vineet Kosaraju, William Saunders, et al. 2021. WebGPT: Browser-assisted question-answering with human feedback. *arXiv preprint arXiv:2112.09332*.

Menaka Narayanan, Emily Chen, Jeffrey He, Been Kim, Sam Gershman, and Finale Doshi-Velez. 2018. How do humans understand explanations from machine learning systems? An evaluation of the human-interpretability of explanation. *arXiv preprint arXiv:1802.00682*.

Richard Yuanzhe Pang, Alicia Parrish, Nitish Joshi, Nikita Nangia, Jason Phang, Angelica Chen, Vishakh Padmakumar, Johnny Ma, Jana Thompson, He He, et al. 2021. QuALITY: Question Answering with Long Input Texts, Yes! *arXiv preprint arXiv:2112.08608*.

Nazneen Fatema Rajani, Bryan McCann, Caiming Xiong, and Richard Socher. 2019. Explain yourself! Leveraging language models for commonsense reasoning. In *Proceedings of the 57th Annual Meeting of the Association for Computational Linguistics*, pages 4932–4942, Florence, Italy. Association for Computational Linguistics.

Philipp Schmidt and Felix Biessmann. 2019. Quantifying interpretability and trust in machine learning systems. *arXiv preprint arXiv:1901.08558*.

Rowan Zellers, Yonatan Bisk, Ali Farhadi, and Yejin Choi. 2019. From recognition to cognition: Visual commonsense reasoning. In *2019 IEEE/CVF Conference on Computer Vision and Pattern Recognition (CVPR)*, pages 6713–6724.

A Writing Task Details

Writer Recruitment We list our task on the freelancing platform Upwork as a writing job open to all workers. We received 112 applications and selected 26 of the most qualified writers to complete a qualification task (2 chose not to complete the qualification). The 24 writers who finish the qualification task are paid $36.00 to complete (i) a tutorial task that consists of a full passage and 10 example arguments with supporting text snippets and explanations about how each argument is constructed, followed by (ii) a qualification task that consists of reading a new passage and constructing 10 arguments with supporting text snippets. Each submission is evaluated on a numeric scale by two of the authors and rated for how convincing the argument is, how useful the snippets are, and how closely the argument needs to be read to select that answer or exclude the other answer option (in order to make sure the writers can construct clear and concise arguments). We aggregate these results for each writer by z-scoring the ratings by each evaluator's scores, and then averaging across questions for each metric. We select the top-performing 14 writers to continue on to the main writing task.

Pay and Bonus Structure We pay writers a base rate of $18 per passage. As it is more difficult to write a convincing explanation for an incorrect answer compared to a correct one, we award writers a bonus of $0.10 for each time a judge selects their argument for a correct answer and $0.50 for each time a judge selects their argument for an incorrect answer option. Which answer option is correct and which one is incorrect is not revealed to the writers during the writing task; they only see this information once they receive feedback about how the judges performed, at which point they find out how much of a bonus they earned.

As stated in the main text, each passage in our final dataset has 7–15 2-option multiple choice questions (avg. of 13.3). However, in the full task given to writers, they constructed arguments for 11-15 questions per passage (average 14.2), but we later determined from metadata in QuALITY that some questions were ambiguous, and we removed those questions from the dataset.

Each multiple choice question is judged by 5 different crowdworkers (see Appendix F for information on these judges), and the average bonus rate per passage is $7.43 (range $2.90 - $15.30), for an effective average hourly rate[4] of $21.04/hr after taking into account Upwork fees.[5]

B Writer Interface

The interface for writers includes a dashboard where the writer can view the passages that we assign them, along with a progress bar for that batch of work. Each passage contains a pane with the full passage and another pane with the questions with both answer options. Writers select text snippets by highlighting the relevant portion of the passage and clicking an 'add snippet' button. Writers are restricted from writing arguments longer than 500 characters or text snippets longer than 250 characters to encourage conciseness and to ensure that judges will be able to read the arguments within the time limit. The writer must both write an argument and select at least one text snippet for each answer. In order to keep the method of referencing text snippets as consistent as possible across different writers with the ultimate goal of being able to train an LM to generate similar arguments, we instruct the writers that they should reference the snippets they select in a uniform way, by either referring to the argument as '#1' or by placing the argument number in parentheses after the relevant part of the argument, as if it were a citation.

Once all the arguments have gone through the judging phase, the writers can view the feedback via their dashboard to see how each of their arguments performed. This dashboard lists how many judges from the PSA condition chose their argument, along with how much of a bonus they earned. This feedback remains available to the writers as they write the next round of arguments.

C Judging Task Crowdworker Recruitment

We recruit judges via Amazon Mechanical Turk (MTurk) using a question-answering qualification task that is open to workers with at least a 98% HIT approval rating and at least 5000 HITs completed; this task pays $2, with a bonus of $1 for anyone

[4]We estimate it takes one hour to complete each passage based on pilot runs and discussion with the writers

[5]Unlike other crowdsourcing platforms like MTurk, Upwork charges fees on the worker's end, and these fees change depending on how much has already been paid to that worker.

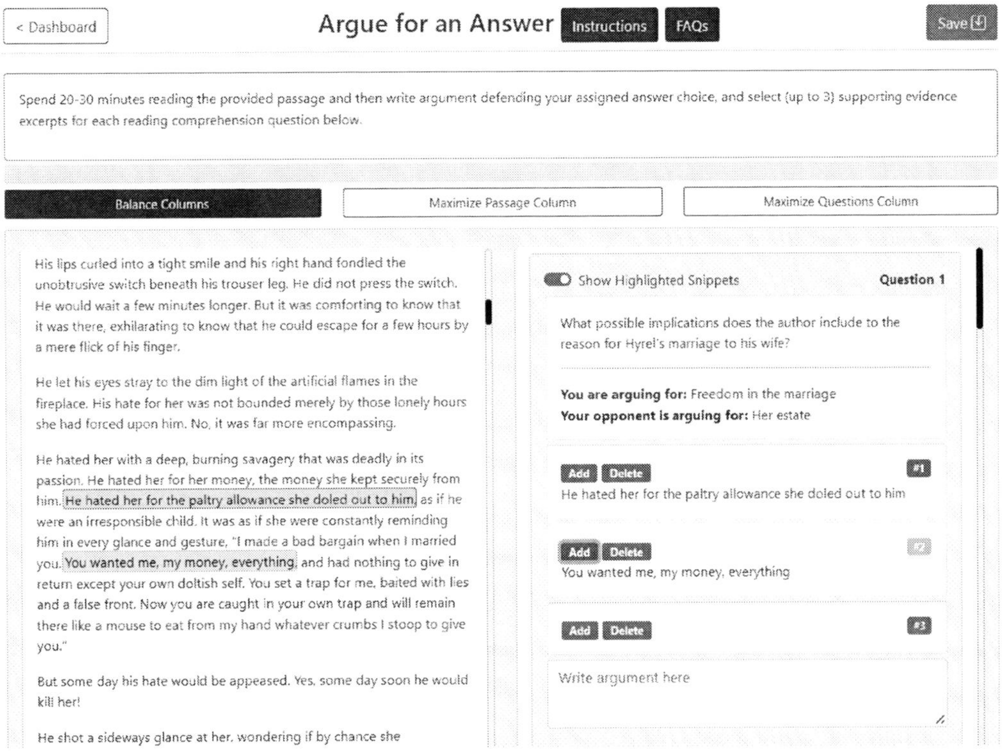

Figure 2: Argument writing interface. In this example, two text snippets have been selected for Question 1.

who passes, and takes approximately 8-10 minutes to complete. In this task, workers read 5 passages of 105–184 words and then answer 2 four-option multiple choice questions about each. A total of 400 workers complete this task, and 249 of them achieve an accuracy above the threshold of 90%. Of these qualified workers, 194 of them end up completing the main task.

D Judging Interface

Judging interfaces are mostly the same in each condition, and only vary in what information is revealed when a worker hits the 'start timer' button (in addition to corresponding changes in the instructions). Figure 3 shows the state of the UI before a worker starts the timer. At this point, the worker only has access to the question and the two answer options. The worker is unable to select either option before starting the timer.

Figure 4 shows an example from PSA where after clicking 'start timer,' the passage, text snippets, and arguments for each of the two answer options is revealed. As the worker scrolls down, the timer remains visible at the top of the screen. Clicking on any of the text snippets auto-scrolls to the relevant portion of the passage and shows color-coded highlights from the text that match the text snippets under each argument. After selecting an answer, the worker scrolls to the bottom of the screen to hit the 'submit' button.

If the timer runs out and the worker still has not hit the 'submit' button, all the information that was presented when they hit 'start timer' disappears and the worker has 30 additional seconds to select one of the two options and click 'submit,' as shown in Figure 5. If this final timer runs out, the task auto-submits and the response is recorded as having no selection, which we mark as an incorrect response.

E Catch Trials

We use catch trials, tasks that look like the test trials but are specifically constructed to be able to be correctly answered given a short time limit, to assess if workers are paying attention and making an effort in the task. In the P condition, the catch trials are taken from the ones used in QuALITY that were constructed to be answerable within one minute by skimming the passage or using a search function (e.g., they include a direct quote that can be searched for with an in-browser search

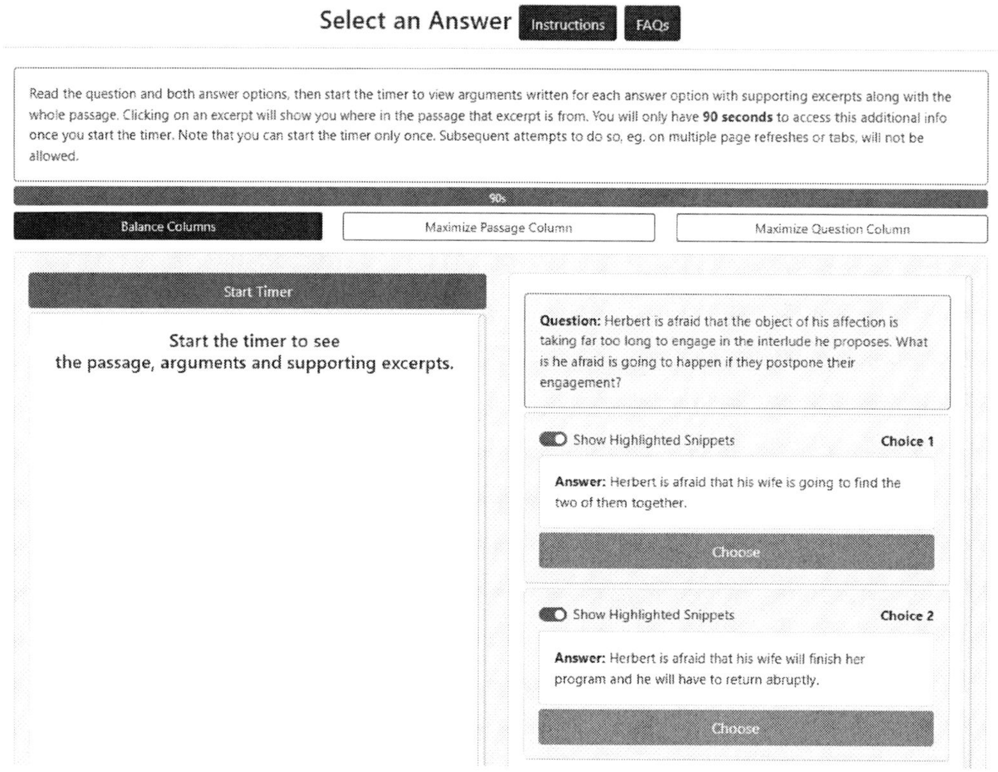

Figure 3: Judging UI before starting the 90s timer.

function like ctrl+F). In the PS and PSA conditions, we construct catch trials by mismatching the argument and/or snippet from another question in that passage onto the incorrect answer option. In this way, it should be obvious to any worker making a faithful attempt at the task which answer option is correct, as one of them is paired with an unrelated argument and/or set of text snippets.

Throughout data collection, we mix approximately 10% of the tasks with catch trials. In order to determine which workers maintain the qualification to complete more tasks, we continuously monitor accuracy on these catch trials. Once workers have completed at least five catch trials in a given condition, if their accuracy on these falls below 60%, we prevent them from completing any more tasks. Although this method relies on workers having already completed a significant number of tasks before we have enough data to dynamically restrict them, this does not seem to be a major concern in data quality because (i) very few workers (6.2%) end up losing the qualification for the task because of low catch trial accuracy, and (ii) aggregation metrics minimize the effect of a few workers not completing the task felicitously. Among workers who completed at least five catch trials in a given condition, median accuracy on the catch trials is 88.9%, indicating that the catch trials can generally be answered given the strict time limit, and that most participants consistently put an honest effort towards the task.

F Initial Group of Judges

During the writing rounds, we use a smaller set of workers as judges and collect five annotations per example. The responses from these judges are used to calculate the writers' bonuses, and this set-up allows us to test out different time limits.

Crowdworker Recruitment We recruit judges via MTurk in two phases. First, we release a reading-comprehension-based qualification task open to workers with at least a 98% HIT approval rating and at least 5000 HITs completed; this task pays \$5, with a \$3 bonus for passing the qualification. In this task, workers read a 3500 word passage and then answer 15 four-option multiple choice questions about that passage. A total of

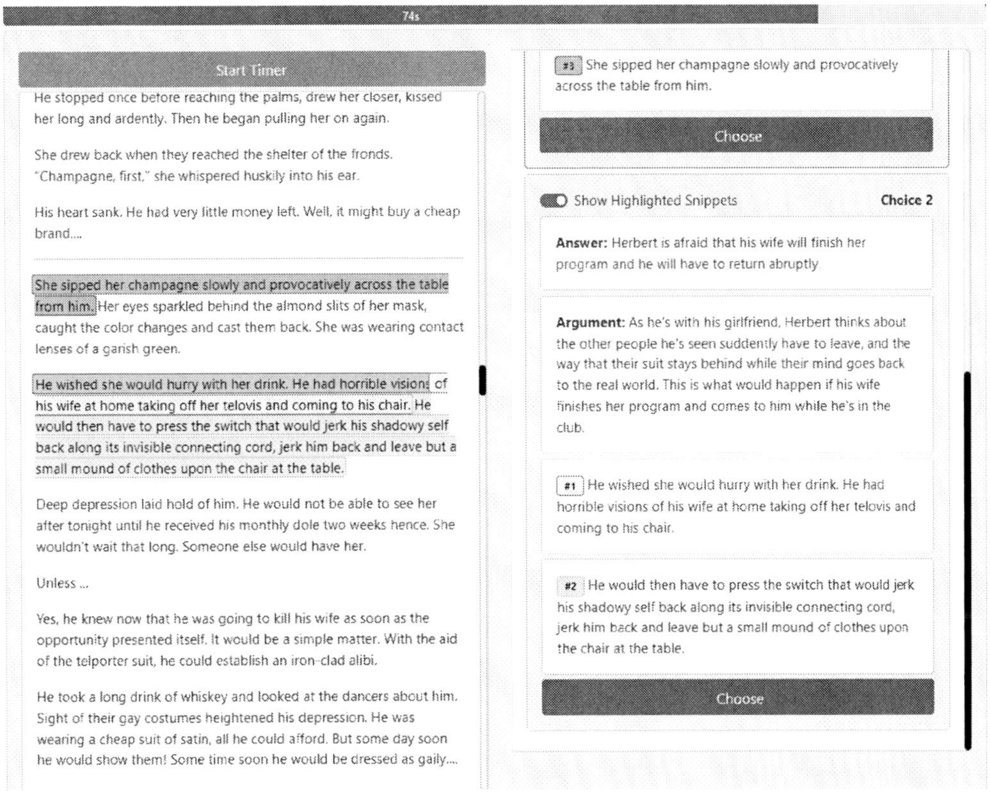

Figure 4: Judging UI after starting the 90s timer. This view shows what happens after someone clicks on one of the text snippets for argument 2 and gets taken to the relevant portion of the text, with that part of the text highlighted.

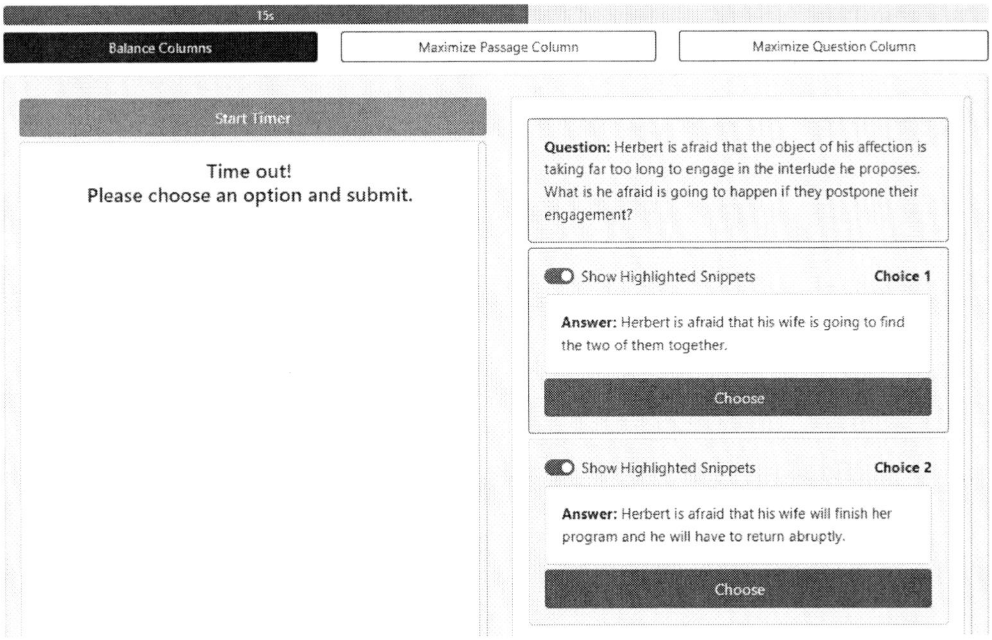

Figure 5: Judging UI after the 90s timer has run out. The arguments, snippets, and text have disappeared, and the judge has only 30 seconds to select a final answer.

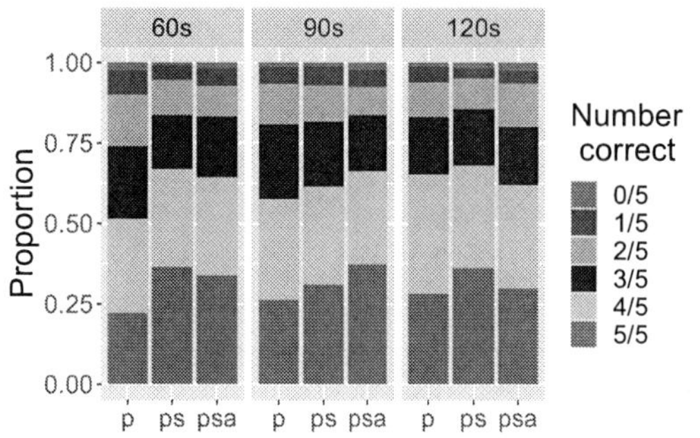

Figure 6: Proportion of pilot judges who answered the question correctly for items within different time limits.

140 workers completed this task, and 77 of them achieved an accuracy above the threshold of 85%.

For the second phase of the qualification, workers complete a timed judging tasks with an upsampled number of catch trials. Sixty-eight of the qualified workers completed at least 24 HITs in this second qualification and were considered for inclusion in the main protocol. In order to pass this second qualification, workers need to achieve above chance accuracy on the test trials in at least two of the three protocols, and they need to answer no more than one catch trial incorrectly. Based on these cutoffs, we qualify 57 crowdworkers to move on to the main judging task, and we pay them an additional $3 bonus. A total of 55 of these workers chose to then take part in the main task, and 42 completed tasks in all three rounds of data collection.

Results with Different Time Limits During the first round of data collection, we use a 60-second time limit, but we raise this limit to 90 seconds for half of the examples in the second round after feedback from workers indicated that several people in the PSA condition did not feel they had sufficient time to read the arguments. This change resulted in only a very small accuracy increase (see Figure 6), so in the third round, we further raise the time limit for half of the questions to 120 seconds, and keep the 90-second limit for the other half of the questions. However, the accuracy increase with longer time limits is most pronounced in P, and so we conclude that performance in PSA in particular is likely not strongly driven by how much time workers have to read the arguments.

Condition	Incorrect selection	Accuracy (%)
P	both	68.0
P	time-limited only	70.2
P	untimed only	62.5
PS	both	73.3
PS	time-limited only	74.0
PS	untimed only	72.3
PSA	both	71.7
PSA	time-limited only	71.2
PSA	untimed only	67.7

Table 2: Accuracy split by the way the incorrect answer option was selected from among three possible options.

G Effect of Question Selection Method

As the incorrect answer option was selected based on whether that option was a good distractor in the time-limited validation used by Pang et al. (2021) *or* based on whether validators who had read the entire passage found that option to be the best distractor, we examine the effect of these two different ways of selecting the incorrect answer option. In about half of the examples, the incorrect option matched both of these criteria. Table 2 shows that workers are slightly less accurate on questions that were selected as the best distractor by the untimed validators (the ones who had read the entire passage). As this difference in accuracy is present in all three conditions and is not more pronounced in PSA compared to the other conditions, it is unlikely that this difference is due to the writers being able to construct a better argument for these questions.

It's worth noting that we would expect the opposite effect of what we observe for P, as this condition is identical to the time-limited task used by Pang et al. (2021), with the caveat that they showed workers four answer options and those workers had even less time to search the passage. We do not have a compelling explanation for this result, though it may be that having given workers more time and fewer options to select from allowed them to more accurately identify the answer in these cases because they had more time to search for the answer and had two fewer answer options, which reduced the number of words to use as search terms and made the task substantially easier. However, this explanation does not account for why accuracy on the questions selected based on QuALITY's time-limited task is the *highest*.

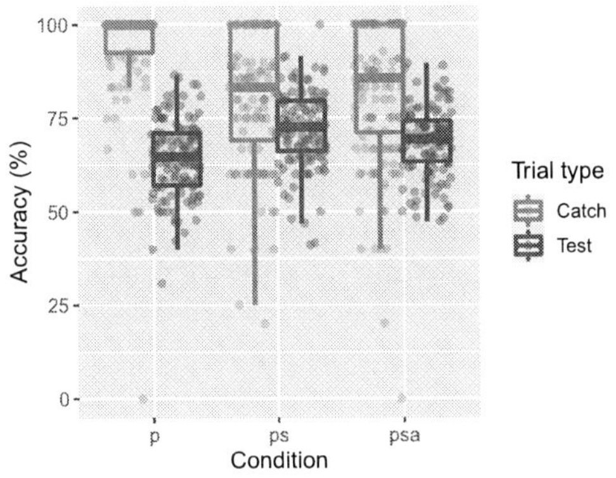

Figure 7: Accuracy of each worker who completed at least 10 tasks in each of the three conditions.

H Per-Worker Results

We observe a great deal of individual variation among workers. It is likely that some people are better at figuring out what words they need to search for to determine the answer, and there is likely variation in how much workers were able to pick up on patterns that would help them answer correctly. This variation seems tied to individual variation more than noise from easier vs. harder questions, as we find that an individual's performance in each condition is significantly predictive of their performance in the other conditions, indicating the workers who did well in, for example, P, were also likely to do well in PS and PSA (P-PS: $r = 0.3$; P-PSA: $r = 0.43$; PS-PSA: $r = 0.15$).

I Additional Results

Improvements Over Time Figure 8 shows the workers' accuracy as they complete more tasks within each condition. We analyze results for workers who did at least 50 tasks in a given condition. As workers get more familiar with each condition, their accuracy improves by a total of about four percentage points. The effect is similar across conditions, and most of the accuracy gains occur after the first 20 tasks completed.

Accuracy by Time Spent on Tasks Figure 9 shows the relationship between how long each worker spent, on average, completing each task and how accurate the worker was. Though there is a very slight positive correlation between time spent and accuracy in PSA, the effect is not statistically significant.

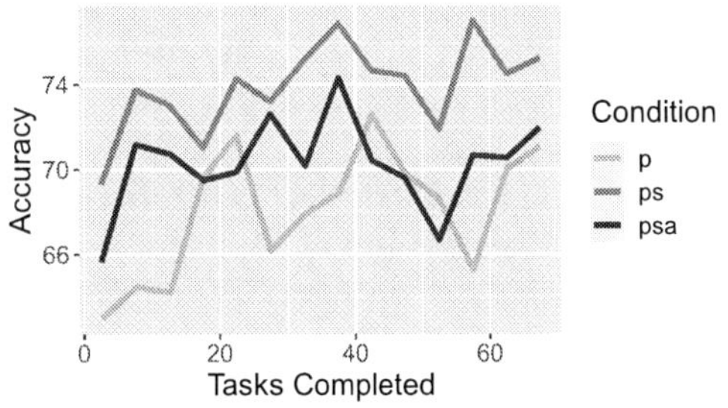

Figure 8: Binned accuracy within each condition, sorted by the order in which each worker completed the tasks. Accuracy improves slightly over time within each condition.

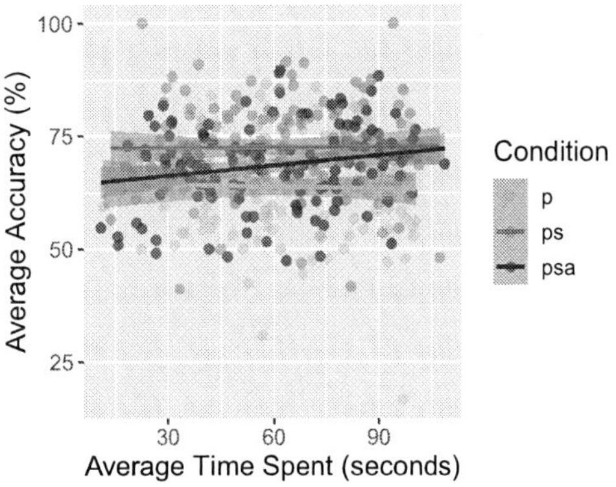

Figure 9: Each worker's average accuracy in each condition, plotted by the average time they spent on each task in that condition. There is no clear advantage to spending more time on the task

Length of Arguments and Snippets Workers are slightly more likely to choose a longer argument. We fit a linear model to predict the rate at which workers choose an answer option from the length of the argument associated with that option in each condition. The effect is small, only about a 1.2 percentage point increase in the rate of choosing that option for every 10 additional words in the argument in PSA relative to the rate of choosing the same option in P, but the effect is significant (p = 0.001).[6] Workers are also more likely to choose an answer option supported by more snippets. For each additional snippet, there is an increase of 4.2 percentage points in the rate at which workers in PSA choose that option, and an increase of 2.8 points in PS (both effects are significantly different from the analogous answer selection rates in P, $p <$ 0.001 and $p = 0.01$, respectively).

Effective Argument Words We check the most common unigrams within correct arguments, and we find no difference between arguments that were chosen 0, 1, 2, or 3 times by the judges. In each case, the four most common words are from within the following set of five words: *earth, time, people, ship, planet.*[7] Similarly, the most common bigrams are not frequent enough to be informative, and are often phrases like *time travel* or *main character*. We also calculate the pointwise mutual information (PMI) of each word within correct and incorrect arguments and within effective and ineffective arguments in order to determine if there are likely to be any lexical regularities workers can pick up on, but no clear trend emerges, and there are numerous ties for words with the highest PMI in each group, even after applying a frequency threshold.

Survey Results Discussion: Mistrust Workers are fairly split in whether they found the arguments helpful or generally mistrusted them. Though the responses in this survey about the arguments are not predictive of accuracy in any of the three conditions, the responses are useful for considering the more psychological effects of presenting people with arguments we know to be false. Having been misled by a convincing-sounding explanation could cause workers to second guess their intuitions and to only rely on information that is grounded in the passage (i.e., the text snippets). In the survey, nearly a quarter of workers explicitly report mistrusting *and then choosing to ignore* the arguments (51 report choosing to use them, 21 say they either chose not to use the arguments from the beginning or changed tactics halfway through after finding the arguments too misleading, and 19 give responses that can't be coded as either generally trustful/mistrustful). Although adopting a stance of general mistrust for the arguments is a logical (and perhaps desirable) strategy, the subsequent decision to ignore the arguments entirely due to this mistrust was an unintended consequence of our design.

[6]There's no significant difference in argument length based on whether it's arguing for a correct or incorrect answer option.

[7]The majority of the context passages were science fiction stories, so these words are expected to come up quite often, relative to their use in other contexts.

When Can Models Learn From Explanations?
A Formal Framework for Understanding the Roles of Explanation Data

Peter Hase and **Mohit Bansal**
Department of Computer Science
University of North Carolina at Chapel Hill
{peter, mbansal}@cs.unc.edu

Abstract

Many methods now exist for conditioning models on task instructions and user-provided explanations for individual data points. These methods show great promise for improving task performance of language models beyond what can be achieved by learning from individual (x, y) pairs. In this paper, we (1) provide a formal framework for characterizing approaches to learning from explanation data, and (2) we propose a synthetic task for studying how models learn from explanation data. In the first direction, we give graphical models for the available modeling approaches, in which explanation data can be used as model *inputs*, as *targets*, or as a *prior*. In the second direction, we introduce a carefully designed synthetic task with several properties making it useful for studying a model's ability to learn from explanation data. Each data point in this binary classification task is accompanied by a string that is essentially an answer to the *why* question: "why does data point x have label y?" (Miller, 2019). We aim to encourage research into this area by identifying key considerations for the modeling problem and providing an empirical test bed for theories of how models can best learn from explanation data.[1]

1 Introduction

A long line of past work has sought to use free-text explanations, rationales, and other similar data to improve machine learning models. Proposed methods use explanations to constrain or regularize the learned model (Zaidan et al., 2007; Small et al., 2011; Ba et al., 2015; Zhang et al., 2016; Srivastava et al., 2017; Liang et al., 2020), to automatically label data for data augmentation (Hancock et al., 2018; Wang et al., 2019a; Awasthi et al., 2020), as additional supervision (Narang et al., 2020; Hase et al., 2020; Pruthi et al., 2021) or intermediate structured variables (Camburu et al., 2018; Rajani et al., 2019; Wiegreffe et al., 2020), and simply as model inputs (Rupprecht et al., 2018; Co-Reyes et al., 2019; Zhou et al., 2020).

Illustrative Example #1

$\mathcal{T}$: When asked for travel times, give them in terms of travel by car.

x: How many hours does it take to travel from Addis Ababa to Dessie?

y: About 8 hours.

e: Addis Ababa and Dessie are 400km apart by road, and assuming you could average 50kph in a car, the travel time would be about 8 hours.

Illustrative Example #2

$\mathcal{T}$: What are the names of people in the text?

x: She was in particular interested in Babbage's work on the Analytical Engine. Lovelace first met him in June 1833, through their mutual friend, and her private tutor, Mary Somerville.

y: Babbage, Lovelace, Mary Somerville.

e: Names will refer to people, who can work on things, meet others, and be tutors. Not all capitalized things are names. Engines are not people, and here June is a date.

Figure 1: Hypothetical data and explanations. Here, x is an input that one might expect a model to produce the correct output for after fitting to (x, y) pairs. For some models, x may be sufficient, while others may benefit from additional information provided by e.

However, there are many tasks in NLP where improvements in performance prove elusive even when using thousands of explanations as additional data (Narang et al., 2020; Hase et al., 2020). A few observations could explain this situation: (1) the modeling space has not been fully explored for these tasks, but improvements are possible; (2) pretrained language models already store the knowledge that the explanations would have provided, so they do not need them; (3) the language models do not need any information that is not already learnable from the task's input-output pairs. We do not yet know which explanation is best, and therefore it would be helpful to more deeply understand the motivations behind existing modeling approaches.

In this paper, we (1) present a formal framework for characterizing approaches to learning from explanation data, and (2) we propose a synthetic task for studying how models learn from natural language data. Specifically, we first present graphical

[1]Our code and data are publicly available at: https://github.com/peterbhase/ExplanationRoles. An extended technical report on this topic is available at: https://arxiv.org/abs/2102.02201.

Proceedings of the First Workshop on Learning with Natural Language Supervision, pages 29 - 39

models for various approaches where explanation data is used either as model *inputs*, *targets*, or *priors*, and we characterize existing methods according to these graphical models. Then, based on past results, we suggest which models might be most appropriate for explanation data. Next, we present a synthetic task which shares important properties with NLP tasks involving explanation data. Constructing this task helps us carefully specify the manner in which we expect explanations to be useful to models. We provide simple experimental verification that the task is solvable by existing Transformer models when using explanations as additional data but very difficult to solve without them. Our aim is to outline promising approaches in the area and contribute a concrete test bed to assist others in developing new models for learning from natural language explanations.

2 Formalizing the Roles of Explanations

In what follows, we discuss our framework for modeling with explanations and relevant work (Sec. 2.1), as well as promising approaches for learning from explanations (Sec. 2.2).

What Is an Explanation? We use the term "explanation" to refer to the data one might collect if asking a person to answer the question, "Why does data point x have label y?" This is a formulation of the explanation as an answer to a *why-question* of the kind discussed in Miller (2019). Rather than try to give a formal definition of the kind of data generated from this question, we proceed with some illustrative examples, shown in Fig. 1.

2.1 Formal Framework and Relevant Work

In this section, we lay out our theory of how explanations may be used in modeling a task, in a standard supervised learning setup for obtaining a MAP estimate of model parameters:

$$\hat{\theta} = \arg\max_{\theta} p(\theta|X, Y)$$
$$p(\theta|X, Y) \propto p(Y|X, \theta)p(\theta)$$

where Y is a set of labels for inputs X. We refer to the role of Y in this probabilistic model as the *target*, X as an *input*, and $p(\theta)$ as a *prior*. Below we describe existing approaches to adding explanations into this framework. An overview of the corresponding graphical models is shown in Fig. 2.

Using Explanations as Targets. Explanations are often used as additional supervision (shown

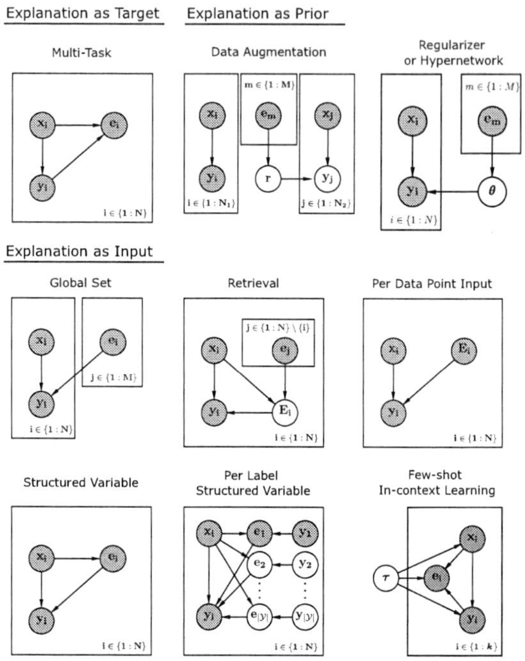

Figure 2: Graphical models for several approaches to using explanations as *targets*, as *inputs*, and as *priors*. Typically past works do not condition on human-given explanations at test time, unless they are designed to not leak the data point label.

as Multi-Task in Fig. 2). For instance, Pruthi et al. (2021) consider using attention weight explanations (from a model) as targets in a multi-task framework, and they observe accuracy improvements in what is essentially model distillation. Meanwhile, natural language explanations appear as targets in a multi-task framework, using datasets with explanations for each data point (Camburu et al., 2018; Narang et al., 2020; Hase et al., 2020; Wiegreffe et al., 2020). None of these works find improvements in task performance from incorporating explanations. It is perhaps even concerning that a model could learn to generate coherent "explanations" without the learning of this ability influencing the models that are found for the task.

Using Explanations as Inputs. Additional inputs may be valuable for solving some tasks. One family of approaches uses explanations as model inputs for each data point (Per Data Point Input in Fig. 2). Talmor et al. (2020) systematically study RoBERTa's ability to combine pieces of knowledge for a task by including relevant factoids in the text input. Co-Reyes et al. (2019) provide online natural language feedback to RL agents, and Rupprecht et al. (2018) take a similar approach to interactive image segmentation with language feedback.

More commonly, approaches do not use human explanations at test time. In ExpBERT (Murty et al., 2020), a model conditions on vector representations of an input x and a single "global" set of explanations in order to make each prediction (Global Set in Fig. 2). This approach may not scale well to large numbers of explanations, however. Zhou et al. (2020) treat explanations as latent variables, and at inference time they retrieve explanations from the training data (Retrieval in Fig. 2). A number of works condition on explanations generated at test time using generative models learned with human explanations as supervision, which are represented as Structured Variable and Per-Label Structured Variable in Fig. 2 (Camburu et al., 2018; Rajani et al., 2019; Kumar and Talukdar, 2020; Hase et al., 2020; Wiegreffe et al., 2020; Zhao and Vydiswaran, 2021). While such structured variables could be useful in principle, these methods have not produced sustained improvements in model accuracy.

Lastly, large language models have recently opened the door for using explanations in few-shot in-context learning (Brown et al., 2020). We represent this approach as Few-shot In-context Learning in Fig. 2. We do not draw the dependencies between distinct data points in the context that would be implied by the attention graph of Transformers, but instead represent the dependence of each data point on the unknown task τ, which models evidently do inference over at test time. Initial work in this direction suggests that models of a sufficiently large size (280B parameters) can learn from explanations provided in a few-shot in-context learning setting (Lampinen et al., 2022).

Using Explanations as Priors. We group together approaches to defining a distribution over model parameters, including those conditioning on data, $p(\theta|data)$. This is a prior over model weights not in the sense that the distribution is independent of data (which it is not), but rather that the posterior parameters are conditioned on the prior. Explanations have been used to constrain the learned model (Srivastava et al., 2017, 2018) or to place priors over how features are weighted or extracted (Zaidan et al., 2007; Small et al., 2011; Zhang et al., 2016; Ross et al., 2017; Bao et al., 2018; Selvaraju et al., 2019; Liang et al., 2020; Stammer et al., 2020; Pruthi et al., 2021; Stacey et al., 2022). Other works map directly from text to model parameters (Ba et al., 2015; Andreas et al., 2018). These methods are all effectively described by Regularizer or Hypernetwork in Fig. 2. Lastly, a few approaches learn to use explanations for automatically labeling data for data augmentation purposes (Hancock et al., 2018; Wang et al., 2019b; Awasthi et al., 2020), which is effectively fitting to data from a prior distribution given by the labeling mechanism (Data Augmentation in Fig. 2).

2.2 Promising Models

Based on our review of existing approaches, we make a few key observations that we believe will assist in the design of future techniques:

1. Using free-text explanations as structured variables and as targets do not appear to be promising approaches at the moment (Hase et al., 2020; Narang et al., 2020).
2. Free-text explanations may be useful as priors in computer vision (Liang et al., 2020), but we know of no successful use case for tasks besides Stacey et al. (2022), which effectively reduces free-text explanations to a bag of words.
3. The only cases we know of where free-text explanations improve model performance on NLP tasks is when they are used as model inputs via the Global Set model, (Murty et al., 2020) a Retrieval model (Zhou et al., 2020), and an In-Context Learning model using 280B parameters (Lampinen et al., 2022).

The upshot of these results is that the most promising approaches for learning from explanation data are likely those treating explanations as inputs (in a manner that does not require new explanations at test time). However, we recommend that other graphical models not be ruled out completely, in case there are promising methods in those families that have yet to be explored.

3 Synthetic Task

Following recent work using synthetic data to investigate sequence modeling questions (Liu et al., 2021; Lovering et al., 2021), we design a synthetic dataset so that we can carefully control several important data properties. In Fig. 3, we show an example data point and description of how it gets its label. The premise of our task is to classify sequences by counting different integers in them.

Core Idea Behind Data. We wish to design a task where, for a data point (x, y), an explanation

Synthetic Task

$\mathcal{T}$: Count whether there are more of integer a than integer b

x: 962 1 80 80 34 40 99 67 50 27 27 17 17 17 17 17 17 53 17 54

y: 1

e: (962, 80, 40, 17, 27)

Description: The sequence x has label 1 because there are more 80s than 40s. The index 962 maps to (80, 40, 17, 27), and indicator 1 says to count (80, 40) rather than (17, 27). If there were more 40s than 80s, the label would be 0. There is a one-to-one map between index values and $e = (index, m, n, r, d)$ tuples.

Analogous Components to Real Data

Index 962 $\leftrightarrow$ An easily computable feature connecting the input to its explanation

Indicator 1 $\leftrightarrow$ A feature indicating what information from the explanation is relevant for the input's label

e: (962, 80, 40, 17, 27) $\leftrightarrow$ An explanation that says why the input received its label, when understood properly

Figure 3: An example of our synthetic task.

e communicates information about *why* input x receives label y. The premise of the task is that a binary label for a sequence of integers x is determined by whether there are more of an integer a in the sequence than there are of an integer b. We refer to integers (a, b) that need to be counted as the *label reason*. This *label reason* forms the basis of the explanation for each data point, and it is always exactly specified by the first two integers in x, which we term the *index* and *indicator*. For every data point x, there is an *explanation* $e = (\textit{index}, m, n, r, d)$ where the *label reason* is given by either (m, n) or (r, d). Whether the *label reason* is the (m, n) integer pair or the (r, d) pair is dictated by the *indicator*. As represented in Fig. 3, $(a, b) = (m, n)$ if the *indicator* is 1 and $(a, b) = (r, d)$ if the *indicator* is 2. We call the data e an explanation because it is a direct encoding of a natural language explanation for the data (x, y). For the data point in Fig. 3, this natural language explanation is "input x receives label 1 because it contains more 80's than 40's, and we do not need to count 17's or 27's for this sequence."

Proposed Dataset. We describe the proposed dataset using some default data parameters for preliminary experiments, but any specific numbers appearing below are easily adjusted. See Supplement D for the full generative process.

1. Train set: 5000 sequences of 20 integers (including *index* and *indicator*), each accompanied by an explanation. There are 500 unique values of *index* in the dataset drawn from $unif(1, 10000)$, so there are 10 points for each *index*, whose values of m, n, r, and d are drawn from $unif(1, 100)$ while requiring that $m \neq n \neq r \neq d$. The corresponding 10 values of *indicator* are split between 1 and 2. Half of the points have label $y{=}1$, i.e. either $\#m > \#n$ or $\#r > \#d$, depending on which feature is causal. In each x_i, after m, n, r, and d have been randomly placed into the sequence, unfilled slots are filled with samples from $unif(1, 100)$.
2. Dev set: 10,000 points, none appearing in Train, with the same 500 *index* values, and twice the number of points per *index* as Train.
3. Test set: 50,000 points of similar construction to the Dev set, but with five times the points per *index* as Train.

Analogous Properties to Human-Curated Data. We claim that aspects of our synthetic task are analogous to properties that natural language data might take on, which we represent in Fig. 3. First, e is an explanation in the sense that, when understood properly, it is a plausible answer to the question: "why does point x have label y?" The explanation describes the feature that causes the label, i.e. the integers that should be counted. We suggest that the *index* in a sequence is analogous to the topic of some text or the things it refers to: it is an easily computable feature that connects the input to the appropriate explanation. Meanwhile, the *indicator* is a feature that tells how information from an explanation is relevant to deciding the label. Similarly, an explanation might only be understood in the context of the input it explains.

4 Initial Experiments

We include experiments below that (1) show explanation data is helpful for solving our task and (2) demonstrate why the task is hard without explanation data. We make use of a retrieval-based model similar to Zhou et al. (2020), which learns to retrieve explanations from the training dataset to help with prediction at test time (details in Appendix B and C). This model is composed of a RoBERTa-base classifier (Liu et al., 2019) and a SentenceRoBERTa model used for retrieval (Reimers and Gurevych, 2019). The baseline in our experiments is the RoBERTa classifer on its own.

4.1 Explanation Retrieval Enables a Model to Solve Our Task

Design. Using our default dataset containing one explanation per training point, we measure model accuracy with retrieval in a 3×2 design. There are three conditions for the retrieval model: (1) *fixed*, where the Sentence-RoBERTa retriever is fixed and only the classifier is trained, (2) *learned*, where both classifier and retriever are trained end-

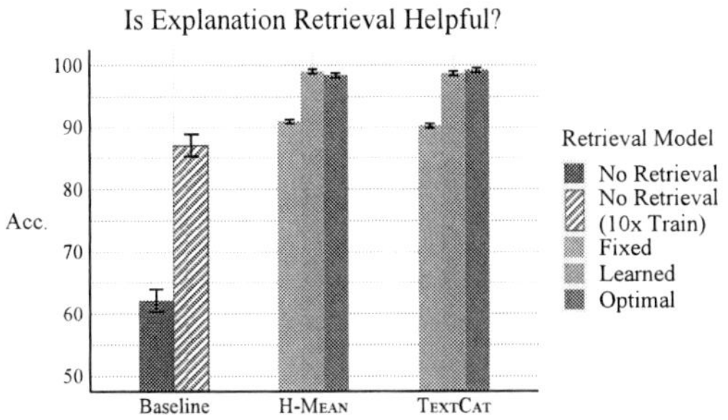

Figure 4: Synthetic task accuracy for our baseline and retrieval model with two conditioning mechanisms, H-MEAN and TEXTCAT.

to-end, and (3) *optimal* where the optimal retrieval model is used and the classifier is trained. We know the optimal retrieval model retrieves explanations with an *index* matching the query point's *index*. The two conditioning mechanisms, H-MEAN and TEXTCAT, differ in how they combine information across multiple retrieved explanations to produce a final prediction (see Appendix B.1).

Results. The results in Fig. 4 show that explanation retrieval can reach accuracies above 98%, improving accuracy by around 37 points over a no-explanation baseline. We also find that the learned retrieval model does as well as the optimal retrieval model, improving over the *fixed* condition by about 7 points. Thus, access to explanations allows the model to perform much better than a no-explanation baseline. In fact, the explanation retrieval model outperforms a no-explanation baseline with as many as 50,000 training data points (a 10x increase), which obtains 87.11% accuracy.

4.2 Why Is The Task Hard Without Explanations?

Design. We measure test accuracy as a function of how many unique explanations (and therefore *label reasons*) there are in the data. While keeping the train set size fixed at 5000 points, we vary how many points share the same explanation ($\textit{index}, m, n, r, d$). By default there are 10 points per *index*, and with 5000 points this means that there are 500 unique explanations in the data. We use many as 2500 points per *index*, meaning using two unique explanations. The experiment conditions also vary in how task information is available in the input: (1) for With Explanation, each 20-integer sequence x_i has its explanation appended to it; (2) for No Explanation, only x_i is given, which requires the model to learn the map

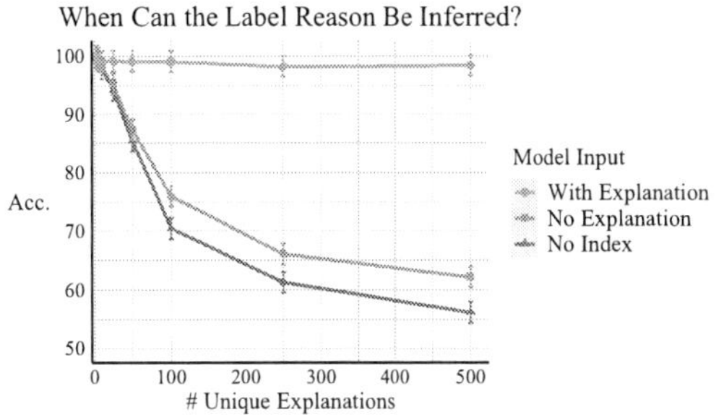

Figure 5: Synthetic task accuracy as a function of the number of unique explanations for data point labels.

index $\rightarrow (m, n, r, d)$; (3) for No Index, the *index* is omitted from the input, so the model must infer the *label reason* from the sequence's contents alone.

Results. The results are shown in Fig. 5. We see that, when the number of unique explanations (and therefore possible *label reasons*) is small, the No Explanation model can achieve an accuracy as high as if it had been directly given the label reason, i.e. as high as the With Explanation condition. Yet, No Explanation model accuracy falls off quickly with the number of unique explanations, reaching accuracies as low as 62.2% with 500 explanations. Evidently, with this many unique explanations, it is too difficult to learn the map between the *index* and the latent *label reason*. Without the *index* in the input (No Index condition), it is even harder to infer the label reason. While accuracy does rise significantly with the size of the training data (see Fig. 4), even using 10x as much train data does not close the gap with the explanation retrieval model.

5 Discussion & Conclusion

We present a synthetic dataset with key similarities to natural language explanation data, and we show that our explanations are highly useful for model learning. However, we emphasize that if a model already "knew" the information in some explanations, it might not need them. This may plausibly occur with sufficiently large pretrained models that store a great deal of factual knowledge (Petroni et al., 2019). Similarly, the necessary information might be learnable from (X, Y) data alone. Future work on modeling approaches we outline in this paper (Fig. 2) will benefit from testing their methods on controlled synthetic tasks as a test of their ability to learn from explanation data. Then, further analysis will be helpful for understanding how explanations contain novel information that is not learned elsewhere in pretraining or finetuning.

Acknowledgements

We thank Miles Turpin and Ethan Perez for helpful discussion of the topics represented here, as well as Xiang Zhou, Prateek Yadav, and our anonymous reviewers for helpful feedback on the work. This work was supported by NSF-CAREER Award 1846185, DARPA Machine-Commonsense (MCS) Grant N66001-19-2-4031, a Google PhD Fellowship, Microsoft Investigator Fellowship, and Google and AWS cloud compute awards. The views contained in this article are those of the authors and not of the funding agency.

Ethical Considerations

There are several positive broader impacts from designing methods for learning from human explanations. Foremost among them is the promise of better aligning learned models with human priors on what kinds of behaviors are good, which could be especially helpful when these priors are hard to robustly encode in supervised learning objectives or unlikely to be learned from the available data. Explanations can also greatly improve model sample efficiency, which is broadly beneficial for difficult, time-consuming, or human-in-the-loop tasks where acquiring a large amount of data is expensive and slow.

There are still some possible risks to this methodology, mainly involving overconfidence in what explanations can provide. For instance, just because explanations improve a model's performance does not mean the model will behave exactly as a human would. We risk anthropomorphizing machine learning models when we suppose their learned interpretations of explanations matches our own.

References

Jacob Andreas, Dan Klein, and Sergey Levine. 2018. Learning with latent language. In *NAACL-HLT 2018*.

Abhijeet Awasthi, Sabyasachi Ghosh, Rasna Goyal, and Sunita Sarawagi. 2020. Learning from rules generalizing labeled exemplars. In *ICLR 2020*.

Lei Jimmy Ba, Kevin Swersky, Sanja Fidler, and Ruslan Salakhutdinov. 2015. Predicting deep zero-shot convolutional neural networks using textual descriptions. In *2015 IEEE International Conference on Computer Vision, ICCV 2015, Santiago, Chile, December 7-13, 2015*, pages 4247–4255. IEEE Computer Society.

Livio Baldini Soares, Nicholas FitzGerald, Jeffrey Ling, and Tom Kwiatkowski. 2019. Matching the blanks: Distributional similarity for relation learning. In *ACL*, pages 2895–2905, Florence, Italy. Association for Computational Linguistics.

Yujia Bao, Shiyu Chang, Mo Yu, and Regina Barzilay. 2018. Deriving machine attention from human rationales. In *EMNLP*, pages 1903–1913, Brussels, Belgium. Association for Computational Linguistics.

Iz Beltagy, Matthew E. Peters, and Arman Cohan. 2020. Longformer: The long-document transformer. *CoRR*, abs/2004.05150.

Tom B. Brown, Benjamin Mann, Nick Ryder, Melanie Subbiah, Jared Kaplan, Prafulla Dhariwal, Arvind Neelakantan, Pranav Shyam, Girish Sastry, Amanda Askell, Sandhini Agarwal, Ariel Herbert-Voss, Gretchen Krueger, Tom Henighan, Rewon Child, Aditya Ramesh, Daniel M. Ziegler, Jeffrey Wu, Clemens Winter, Christopher Hesse, Mark Chen, Eric Sigler, Mateusz Litwin, Scott Gray, Benjamin Chess, Jack Clark, Christopher Berner, Sam McCandlish, Alec Radford, Ilya Sutskever, and Dario Amodei. 2020. Language models are few-shot learners. In *NeurIPS*.

Oana-Maria Camburu, Tim Rocktäschel, Thomas Lukasiewicz, and Phil Blunsom. 2018. e-snli: Natural language inference with natural language explanations. In *NeurIPS 2018*.

John D. Co-Reyes, Abhishek Gupta, Suvansh Sanjeev, Nick Altieri, Jacob Andreas, John DeNero, Pieter Abbeel, and Sergey Levine. 2019. Guiding policies with language via meta-learning. In *ICLR 2019*.

Braden Hancock, Paroma Varma, Stephanie Wang, Martin Bringmann, Percy Liang, and Christopher Ré. 2018. Training classifiers with natural language explanations. In *ACL*.

Peter Hase, Shiyue Zhang, Harry Xie, and Mohit Bansal. 2020. Leakage-adjusted simulatability: Can models generate non-trivial explanations of their behavior in natural language? In *Findings of EMNLP*.

Jeff Johnson, Matthijs Douze, and Hervé Jégou. 2017. Billion-scale similarity search with gpus. *IEEE Transactions on Big Data*.

Vladimir Karpukhin, Barlas Oguz, Sewon Min, Patrick Lewis, Ledell Wu, Sergey Edunov, Danqi Chen, and Wen-tau Yih. 2020. Dense passage retrieval for open-domain question answering. In *EMNLP*, pages 6769–6781, Online. Association for Computational Linguistics.

Sawan Kumar and Partha Talukdar. 2020. Nile : Natural language inference with faithful natural language explanations. In *ACL 2020*.

Andrew K Lampinen, Ishita Dasgupta, Stephanie CY Chan, Kory Matthewson, Michael Henry Tessler, Antonia Creswell, James L McClelland, Jane X

Wang, and Felix Hill. 2022. Can language models learn from explanations in context? *arXiv preprint arXiv:2204.02329*.

Patrick S. H. Lewis, Ethan Perez, Aleksandra Piktus, Fabio Petroni, Vladimir Karpukhin, Naman Goyal, Heinrich Küttler, Mike Lewis, Wen-tau Yih, Tim Rocktäschel, Sebastian Riedel, and Douwe Kiela. 2020. Retrieval-augmented generation for knowledge-intensive NLP tasks. In *NeurIPS*.

Weixin Liang, James Zou, and Zhou Yu. 2020. ALICE: active learning with contrastive natural language explanations. In *EMNLP*, pages 4380–4391. Association for Computational Linguistics.

Nelson F. Liu, Tony Lee, Robin Jia, and Percy Liang. 2021. Can small and synthetic benchmarks drive modeling innovation? a retrospective study of question answering modeling approaches. *CoRR*.

Yinhan Liu, Myle Ott, Naman Goyal, Jingfei Du, Mandar Joshi, Danqi Chen, Omer Levy, Mike Lewis, Luke Zettlemoyer, and Veselin Stoyanov. 2019. Roberta: A robustly optimized bert pretraining approach. *ArXiv*, abs/1907.11692.

Charles Lovering, Rohan Jha, Tal Linzen, and Ellie Pavlick. 2021. Predicting inductive biases of pretrained models.

Tim Miller. 2019. Explanation in artificial intelligence: Insights from the social sciences. *Artif. Intell.*, 267:1–38.

Shikhar Murty, Pang Wei Koh, and Percy Liang. 2020. Expbert: Representation engineering with natural language explanations. In *ACL*, pages 2106–2113. Association for Computational Linguistics.

Sharan Narang, Colin Raffel, Katherine J. Lee, Adam Roberts, Noah Fiedel, and Karishma Malkan. 2020. WT5?! training text-to-text models to explain their predictions. *ArXiv*, abs/2004.14546.

Fabio Petroni, Tim Rocktäschel, Sebastian Riedel, Patrick Lewis, Anton Bakhtin, Yuxiang Wu, and Alexander Miller. 2019. Language models as knowledge bases? In *Proceedings of the 2019 Conference on Empirical Methods in Natural Language Processing and the 9th International Joint Conference on Natural Language Processing (EMNLP-IJCNLP)*, pages 2463–2473, Hong Kong, China. Association for Computational Linguistics.

Danish Pruthi, Bhuwan Dhingra, Livio Baldini Soares, Michael Collins, Zachary C. Lipton, Graham Neubig, and William W. Cohen. 2021. Evaluating explanations: How much do explanations from the teacher aid students? *TACL*, abs/2012.00893.

Nazneen Fatema Rajani, Bryan McCann, Caiming Xiong, and Richard Socher. 2019. Explain yourself! leveraging language models for commonsense reasoning. In *ACL 2019*.

Nils Reimers and Iryna Gurevych. 2019. Sentence-BERT: Sentence embeddings using Siamese BERT-networks. In *EMNLP-IJCNLP*, pages 3982–3992, Hong Kong, China. Association for Computational Linguistics.

Andrew Slavin Ross, Michael C. Hughes, and Finale Doshi-Velez. 2017. Right for the right reasons: Training differentiable models by constraining their explanations. In *IJCAI*, pages 2662–2670.

Christian Rupprecht, Iro Laina, Nassir Navab, Gregory D. Harger, and Federico Tombari. 2018. Guide me: Interacting with deep networks. In *Proceedings of the IEEE Conference on Computer Vision and Pattern Recognition, CVPR 2018*.

Ramprasaath Ramasamy Selvaraju, Stefan Lee, Yilin Shen, Hongxia Jin, Shalini Ghosh, Larry P. Heck, Dhruv Batra, and Devi Parikh. 2019. Taking a HINT: leveraging explanations to make vision and language models more grounded. In *ICCV*, pages 2591–2600. IEEE.

Kevin Small, Byron C Wallace, Carla E Brodley, and Thomas A Trikalinos. 2011. The constrained weight space svm: learning with ranked features. In *ICML*, pages 865–872.

Shashank Srivastava, I. Labutov, and T. Mitchell. 2017. Learning classifiers from declarative language. In *NeurIPS 2017*.

Shashank Srivastava, Igor Labutov, and Tom Mitchell. 2018. Zero-shot learning of classifiers from natural language quantification. In *ACL 2018*.

Joe Stacey, Yonatan Belinkov, and Marek Rei. 2022. Supervising model attention with human explanations for robust natural language inference. In *AAAI*.

Wolfgang Stammer, Patrick Schramowski, and Kristian Kersting. 2020. Right for the right concept: Revising neuro-symbolic concepts by interacting with their explanations. *CoRR*, abs/2011.12854.

Alon Talmor, Oyvind Tafjord, Peter Clark, Yoav Goldberg, and Jonathan Berant. 2020. Leap-of-thought: Teaching pre-trained models to systematically reason over implicit knowledge. In *NeurIPS 2020*.

Cunxiang Wang, Shuailong Liang, Yue Zhang, Xiaonan Li, and Tian Gao. 2019a. Does it make sense? and why? a pilot study for sense making and explanation. In *ACL 2019*.

Ziqi Wang, Yujia Qin, Wenxuan Zhou, Jun Yan, Qinyuan Ye, Leonardo Neves, Zhiyuan Liu, and Xiang Ren. 2019b. Learning from explanations with neural execution tree. In *ICLR*.

Sarah Wiegreffe, Ana Marasovic, and Noah A. Smith. 2020. Measuring association between labels and free-text rationales. *CoRR*, abs/2010.12762.

Omar Zaidan, Jason Eisner, and Christine Piatko. 2007. Using "Annotator Rationales" to Improve Machine Learning for Text Categorization. In *Human Language Technologies 2007: The Conference of the North American Chapter of the Association for Computational Linguistics; Proceedings of the Main Conference*, pages 260–267, Rochester, New York. Association for Computational Linguistics.

Ye Zhang, Iain Marshall, and Byron C. Wallace. 2016. Rationale-Augmented Convolutional Neural Networks for Text Classification. In *Proceedings of the 2016 Conference on Empirical Methods in Natural Language Processing*, pages 795–804, Austin, Texas. Association for Computational Linguistics.

Xinyan Zhao and VG Vydiswaran. 2021. Lirex: Augmenting language inference with relevant explanation. In *AAAI*.

Wangchunshu Zhou, Jinyi Hu, Hanlin Zhang, Xiaodan Liang, Maosong Sun, Chenyan Xiong, and Jian Tang. 2020. Towards interpretable natural language understanding with explanations as latent variables. In *NeurIPS*.

A Additional Experiments

We give additional experimental results with our synthetic dataset in an extended technical report on this topic, available here: `https://arxiv.org/abs/2102.02201`. Additional experiments are conducted to answer a research questions including:

1. Can explanations help models learn to use strong (causal, generalizable) features rather than weak ones?
2. What is the best way to compute explanation representations for prediction?
3. Can models aggregate information across several retrieved explanations?
4. What makes an explanation relevant across data points? What enables a retrieval model to find relevant explanations for a new data point?
5. How does the co-dependence between classifier and retrieval model influence the viability of joint training?
6. Does retrieval of explanations improve model performance on existing natural language datasets?

B Our Model for Initial Experiments

Here, we introduce our chosen model for incorporating explanation data, which makes use of explanations as *model inputs* after they are retrieved from the training data (the "Retrieval" graphical model in Fig. 2). Our approach is similar to Lewis et al. (2020), who marginalize over latent documents retrieved from Wikipedia for question answering, question generation, and fact verification. The marginal distribution is given as:

$$p_\Theta(y|x) = \sum_{e \in \text{top-}k(p_\eta(\cdot|x))} p_\theta(y|x,e)p_\eta(e|x)$$

where top-k gets the top k texts as ranked by the retrieval model, $p_\eta(e|x)$. Note that we never retrieve a data point's own explanation when predicting its label. We do so because explanations can leak the label (Hase et al., 2020) and this approach matches the test-time distribution, where we assume explanations are not collected for new data points (see discussion in Sec. 2).

Zhou et al. (2020) also propose to use explanations as latent variables and retrieve explanations at inference time, but they do not learn the retrieval model, marginalize over the latents during inference, or prohibit data point's own explanations from being retrieved. In our experiments, we compare with their original approach and a version where we marginalize over the latents and learn the retrieval model.

The form of $p_\eta(e|x)$ follows Lewis et al. (2020) and Karpukhin et al. (2020). Given a query x, unnormalized probabilities are computed as:

$$p_\eta(e|x) \propto \exp\left(f_\eta(e)^T f_\eta(x)\right)$$

where f_η embeds each sequence into a vector. To compute top-$k(p_\eta(\cdot|x))$, we search through the training explanations using FAISS (Johnson et al., 2017). We discuss methods for computing $p_\theta(y|x,e)$ and $f_\eta(e|x)$ in Sec. B.1. Because it may be helpful to reason over multiple explanations at once, we extend this model to allow for explanations to be composed into a single "document." Assuming explanations to be conditionally independent given x, we can compute the probability of a set of explanations $E = \{e_c\}_{c=1}^C$ as

$$p(E|x) \propto \exp\left(\sum_{e \in E} f_\eta(e)^T f_\eta(x)\right),$$

where (1) a *context size* C will control the size of the explanation set, (2) a value of k implies that the top Ck will be retrieved, and (3) we sort these Ck explanations into sets in order of their probability $p_\eta(e|x)$.

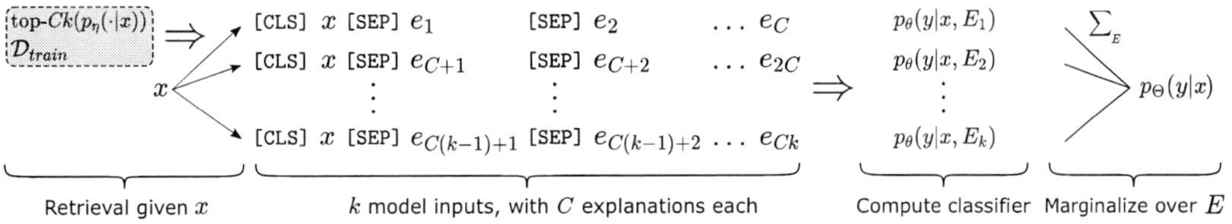

Figure 6: A depiction of our retrieval-based method TEXTCAT. A total of Ck explanations are retrieved and allocated into k latent variables, each a set of explanations E, which are marginalized over to produce a final prediction.

We represent the overall approach in Fig. 6 for one method of computing $p_\theta(y|x, E)$ (described fully in Sec. B.1), where explanations are concatenated with the query sequence. Flowing from left to right, Fig. 6 shows how explanations are retrieved from the training data conditioned on a query sequence x, then allocated into k classifier inputs with C explanations each. The k classifier predictions are aggregated by marginalizing over the latent variable, $Z = E$.

Modeling Assumptions. In using retrieval, we make a few assumptions. First, since the number of forward passes per data point scales with k, we require a relatively small value of k, i.e. $k \leq 10$, for reasonable computational efficiency in SGD-based training. Hence, we must assume that this summation is sufficiently similar to the full summation over latent variables. This assumption is more likely to hold when (1) a small number of documents account for most of the probability mass in $p_\eta(e|x)$, and (2) a pretrained model $p_\eta(e|x)$ yields a decent initial rank-ordering, such that some of the best documents are in the top-k. The exact value of k we use depends on the experiment. A second, more basic assumption is that explanations will be useful in predicting other data points' labels. Such an assumption is needed since we never condition on a data point's own explanation. Lastly, during retrieval we assume that explanations are independent given x, i.e. $p(E|x) = \prod_{e \in E} p(e|x)$. This could be a poor assumption when, for instance, explanations each contribute one of a number of needed facts, in which case it would be helpful to retrieve additional explanations conditioned on what has already been retrieved.

B.1 Conditioning Mechanisms

In this section we describe the methods used to compute $p_\theta(y|x, E)$ and $p_\eta(e|x)$ (see Sec. B for the overall model description). For the classifier $p_\theta(y|x, E)$, we use two methods, TEXTCAT and H-MEAN, which are described below. Then we describe the retrieval model, which is based on Sentence-BERT (Reimers and Gurevych, 2019).

TEXTCAT. Represented in Figure 6, this method takes a straightforward approach to conditioning on a set of explanations: concatenating C explanations and the input x to form a longer sequence of text. Each of the original sequences is separated by a special token, e.g. [SEP] for BERT. In our experiments, we pass this longer sequence into a RoBERTa-base model. After pooling the output token representations, we pass the resulting vector to a 1-layer MLP for classification. We use mean pooling for our synthetic task and NLI; for relation extraction tasks, we concatenate the representations corresponding to the initial tokens in the *subject* and *object* words, since this is an especially effective pooling technique (Baldini Soares et al., 2019).

This approach allows the model to reason over all of the explanations and the input together. While the method may be limited by the fact that some models can face difficulties in processing long pieces of text (Beltagy et al., 2020), this issue is partly mitigated by marginalizing over k sets of explanations. As a result of the marginalization, the final prediction can be conditioned on a far higher number (Ck) of individual explanations than could fit in the context alone.

H-MEAN. By H-MEAN, we refer to the kind of unweighted hidden representation averaging used in Co-Reyes et al. (2019) and Zhou et al. (2020). H-MEAN works by first obtaining representations of the input x and a single explanation e at a time, then passing the unweighted average of these representations to an MLP. For a fair comparison with TEXTCAT, we use the same token pooling and a 1-layer MLP. So with C explanations to condition on, $x' = concatenate(x, e)$, and vector representations from RoBERTa(x'), H-MEAN obtains a single representation as

$$h = \frac{1}{C} \sum_{c=1}^{C} \text{RoBERTa}(x')$$

which is then passed to the MLP for classification. H-MEAN does not face the same sequence length limitations as TEXTCAT, but by separately processing of each explanations H-MEAN may fail to integrate information across explanations. This method also becomes expensive when we marginalize over E (which is what allows retrieval to be learned), as it requires Ck forward passes for a single prediction.

B.2 Retrieval

We use a similar approach to retrieval as in Lewis et al. (2020), namely using vector representations of sequences from a pretrained transformer to compute

$$p_\eta(e|x) \propto \exp\left(f_\eta(e)^T f_\eta(x)\right),$$

which is followed by computing top-$Ck(p_\eta(\cdot|x)$. We use an approximate but sub-linear time search method (FAISS) to find the top-Ck points (Johnson et al., 2017). In our experiments we find that it is necessary to use Sentence-BERT (Reimers and Gurevych, 2019) as our pretrained f_η, rather than simply a pretrained RoBERTa model. Sentence-BERT is a network trained to produce semantic representations of sentences that can be compared under cosine similarity. In our experiments, we use the Sentence-RoBERTa-base model trained on a combination of several NLI and semantic textual similarity tasks, with mean pooling of token representations. We normalize the representations we obtain from this model, so that our inner product is equivalent to a cosine similarity.

Note that during training, we never condition on a data point's own explanation when predicting its label. This is an important constraint for matching the train and test-time distributions. At test time, we assume we have access only to past (training) explanations, since they can be expensive to collect and conditioning on explanations at test time can lead to label leakage, meaning what is essentially the benefit of human labeling could be mistaken as improvements in model performance.

C Training Details

C.1 Runtimes.

Regarding training times, we run most experiments on a single NVIDIA RTX 2080 GPU, with runtimes as follows: 4.0 hours for 40 epochs of the no-retrieval RoBERTa-base using the synthetic dataset; 5.7 hours for 40 epochs of RoBERTa-large in the same setting; 8.6 hours for 20 epochs of learned retrieval with RoBERTa-base models on synthetic data.

C.2 Training Hyperparameters and Analysis

For optimization, we use AdamW with a learning rate of $1\text{e}{-5}$ and gradient norm clipping at norm 1. For the LR, we use a linear warmup and decay schedule peaking at 10% of the training steps for experiments with synthetic data and at 1% for experiments with existing datasets (given the larger training set sizes). The batch size is set to 10 across all experiments.

We decide how often to rebuild the representations of training explanations while learning the retrieval model by tuning across frequency values in the range $\{10\%, 20\%, 33\%, 50\%, 100\%\}$ (i.e. to rebuild at this percentage of every epoch), as well as never rebuilding. In our synthetic setting, the only noticeable drop in performance comes from never rebuilding. As long as representations are re-encoded at least as often as every epoch, we notice no difference in final test accuracy, though in early experiments we observed that rebuilding more often improved training stability. To err on the safe side of training stability, we re-encode the representations every 20% of each epoch in all experiments except e-SNLI with full data, where we re-encode every 30% of each epoch.

Additionally, we use the stop-gradient function when computing the gradient of $p_\eta(e|x)$ as follows:

$$\nabla_\eta \exp\left(\text{sg}[f_\eta(e)]^T f_\eta(x)\right),$$

meaning that we do not differentiate through the explanation embeddings, but only through the query data point embeddings. In early experiments, we found that this decision contributed to training stability, while improving computational efficiency, and we confirm that we observe no differences in model accuracy as a result.

C.3 Experiment Confidence Intervals

We compute confidence intervals for our synthetic data tasks to represent *seed variance* around some mean seed performance. We represent seed variance in figures rather than sample variance because the sample variance is fairly low with 50,000 test points and could be driven arbitrarily low with more generated test points. For instance, the 95% confidence interval for a model accuracy of 90% would be ± 0.26. To calculate seed variance, we run 10 random seeds for our baseline condition (no-retrieval) with the default synthetic task setup.

D Synthetic Task Generative Process

The required parameters to the data generation include: (1) a training sample size *sample-size* and (2) *num-tasks*, the number of unique integer pairs to be counted, or, equivalently, the number of points per *index*, n_{task}. In all experiments, we use a maximum integer value of 100 to appear in the sequences, and a maximum *index* value of 10,000. We give the general generative process below. Note that the dev and test sets are constructed with the extra constraint that sequences must not appear in the training data. Further note that this is the generic version of generative process, and in some experiments the process is altered. For example, in RQ3, *indicator* is always 1 and the construction of the map from *index* values to (m, n) tuples occurs in a special way described in the experimental design for RQ3.

1. Sample $\{index_t\}_{\tau=1}^{num\text{-}tasks}$ from the uniform distribution over integers {1,...,10000} without replacement.

2. Sample $\{(m, n, r, d)_t\}_{\tau=1}^{num\text{-}tasks}$ from the uniform distribution over integers, $unif([1, 100]^4)$, without replacement and requiring that $m \neq n \neq r \neq d$.

3. Define the set $\{(index, m, n, r, d)_{index})\}$ for *index* and (m, n, r, d) drawn from their respective sets, without replacement, in an arbitrary order.

4. Compute the number of points per *index*, $n_{task} = sample\text{-}size \; // \; num\text{-}tasks$.

5. For each $index \in \{index_t\}_{\tau=1}^{num\text{-}tasks}$:
   (a) Sample a vector of length n_{task}, balanced between 1s and 2s, that gives the values of $\{indicator_p\}_{p=1}^{P}$ for the P points with that *index*.
   (b) Sample a vector of length n_{task}, balanced between 0s and 1s, representing whether the features $\mathbb{1}[\#m>\#n]$ and $\mathbb{1}[\#r>\#d]$ should correlate (1 implies they are equal, and 0 unequal). This balance changes when the strong-weak correlation is intended to change.
   (c) Sample a vector of length n_{task}, balanced between 0s and 1s, representing whether (m, n) or (r, d) should be the more *numerous* integers in the sequence (so that there is no bias, even randomly, between features by size).
   (d) For $i \in 1 : n_{task}$:
      i. Place the *index* in the first element of an empty array, and the *indicator* in the second.
      ii. Based on the ith elements of the three vectors described above, allocate samples of the integers in $(m, n, r, d)_{index}$ into the remaining 18 slots.
      iii. If there are any remaining slots after these integers are randomly allocated, fill them with i.i.d. samples from $unif(1, 100)$.

A survey on improving NLP models with human explanations

Mareike Hartmann[1] **Daniel Sonntag**[1,2]
[1]German Research Center for Artificial Intelligence (DFKI), Germany
[2]Applied Artifical Intelligence (AAI), Oldenburg University, Germany
{mareike.hartmann, daniel.sonntag}@dfki.de

Abstract

Training a model with access to human explanations can improve data efficiency and model performance on in- and out-of-domain data. Adding to these empirical findings, similarity with the process of human learning makes learning from explanations a promising way to establish a fruitful human-machine interaction. Several methods have been proposed for improving natural language processing (NLP) models with human explanations, that rely on different explanation types and mechanism for integrating these explanations into the learning process. These methods are rarely compared with each other, making it hard for practitioners to choose the best combination of explanation type and integration mechanism for a specific use-case. In this paper, we give an overview of different methods for learning from human explanations, and discuss different factors that can inform the decision of which method to choose for a specific use-case.

	E-SNLI
Premise	A 2-3 year old **blond** child is kneeling on a couch.
Hypothesis	The child has **brown** hair.
Gold label	`Contradiction`
Free-text	The child would not have brown hair if he/she was blond.
	COS-E
Questions	What would not be true about a basketball if it **had a hole** in it but it did not lose its general shape?
Answer options	a) punctured, b) full of air, c) round
Gold label	`b)`
Free-text	Air cannot stay in any object that has a hole in it.

Table 1: Examples of highlight (words marked in bold) and free-text explanations in the E-SNLI dataset (Camburu et al., 2018) for natural language inference and COS-E dataset (Rajani et al., 2019) for multiple choice question answering.

1 Introduction

Training machine learning models with human explanations is considered a promising way for interaction between human and machine that can lead to better models and happier users. If a model is provided with information about *why* a specific prediction should be made for an instance, it can often learn more and faster than if just given the correct label assignment (Godbole et al., 2004; Zaidan et al., 2007). This reduces the need for annotated data and makes learning from explanations attractive for use-cases with little annotated data available, for example for adapting models to new domains (Yao et al., 2021) or for personalizing them (Kulesza et al., 2015). Human explanations also push models to focus on relevant features of the data, preventing them from fitting to spurious correlations in the data (Teso and Kersting, 2019). On top of these beneficial effects on model quality, supervision in the form of explanations is in line with human preferences, as users asked to give feedback to a model want to provide richer feedback than just correct labels (Stumpf et al., 2007; Amershi et al., 2014; Ghai et al., 2021).

Several approaches for learning from human explanations have been proposed for different tasks (Table 2), relying on different types of explanations (Table 1), and different methods for integrating them into the learning process. In this paper, we review the literature on learning from highlight and free-text explanations for NLP models, listing technical possibilities and identifying and describing factors that can inform the decision for an optimal learning approach that should optimize both model quality and user satisfaction. Our categorization of methods for integrating explanation information (§ 2.1) is similar to the one provided by Hase and Bansal (2021).[1] Whereas their categorization fo-

[1]Their survey of methods has a broader scope than ours and includes works that improve e.g. image processing models, whereas we exclusively focus on improving NLP models.

Proceedings of the First Workshop on Learning with Natural Language Supervision, pages 40 - 47

cuses on contrasting the approaches according to the role of explanation data in the learning process, we focus on how different types of explanations can be integrated with these approaches.

2 Learning from Explanations

Highlight and free-text explanations are the most prominent explanation types used to improve NLP models (Wiegreffe and Marasovic, 2021). *Highlight explanations* (HIGHLIGHT) are subsets of input elements that are deemed relevant for a prediction.[2] For text-based NLP tasks, they correspond to sets of words, phrases or sentences. *Free-text explanations* (FREE-TEXT) are texts in natural language that are not constrained to be grounded in the input elements and contain implicit or explicit information about why an instance is assigned a specific label. Some recent works rely on *semi-structured text explanations* (SEMI-STRUCTURED) (Wiegreffe and Marasovic, 2021), which combine properties of both highlight and free-text explanations. They consist of text in natural language and contain an explicit indication of the input elements that the free-text applies to.[3] If and how much a model can be improved based on such explanations depends on the amount of information contained in the explanation (§ 2.2), and to what extent this information can be integrated into the learning process (§ 2.1). User satisfaction is affected by the effort required to produce explanations and by the difficulty of the task, that might in turn affect explanation quality (§ 2.3). In the following, we discuss these factors in detail and where possible contrast them with respect to explanation type.

Objectives Approaches for learning from explanations have been evaluated with different objectives in mind, and we introduce the different motivations below and link them with their respective evaluation in Table 2 (RESULTS column). Early works for learning from explanations were motivated by making the learning process more *efficient* (EFFICIENCY). Integrating human explanations into the learning process leads to better models trained on the same amount of examples (Zaidan et al., 2007), and to better models trained with annotations collected in the same amount of time (Wang et al., 2020), i.e. human labor can be used more efficiently. This makes the paradigm useful for use-cases that allow the collection of additional annotations. Information contained in human explanations can make the model generalize better and lead to better predictive performance on *out-of-domain data* (OUT-OF-DOMAIN), which is most relevant if the model has to be applied under a distribution shift without access to additional annotations. Even with large amounts of annotated data available, models can fit to noise or unwanted biases in the data (Sun et al., 2019), leading to potentially harmful outcomes. Providing human explanations can prevent a model from fitting to such spurious correlations and reduce bias (BIAS REDUCTION).[4] More recently, human explanations have been used in order to improve model explanations (MODEL EXPLANATION, Strout et al. (2019)) or as targets to enable models to generate explanations in the first place (Wiegreffe et al., 2021).

2.1 Integrating explanation information

We now give an overview of different methods[5] that are most commonly applied for integrating the information contained in the human explanation into the model (METHOD column in Table 2).

Given an input sequence $\mathbf{x} = (x_1, \cdots, x_L)$ of length L, a highlight explanation $\mathbf{a}$ is a sequence of attribution scores $\mathbf{a} = (a_1, \cdots, a_L)$, which is of the same length as $\mathbf{x}$ and assigns an importance of $a_i \in \mathbb{R}$ to input element x_i. In practice, a_i is often binary. A free-text explanation $\mathbf{e} = (e_1, \cdots, e_M)$ is a sequence of words of arbitrary length.

Regularizing feature importance This is the dominant approach for learning from highlight explanations. The model is trained by minimizing an augmented loss function $\mathcal{L} = \mathcal{L}_{\text{CLS}} + \mathcal{L}_{\text{EXP}}$ composed of the standard cross-entropy classification loss $\mathcal{L}_{\text{CLS}}$ and an additional explanation loss $\mathcal{L}_{\text{EXP}}$. Given a sequence $\hat{\mathbf{a}} = (\hat{a}_1, \cdots, \hat{a}_L)$ of attribution scores extracted from the model, the explanation loss is computed by measuring the distance between gold attributions a_i and model attribution $\hat{a}_i$ according to $\mathcal{L}_{\text{EXP}}(\mathbf{a}, \hat{\mathbf{a}}) = \sum_i^L \text{dist}(a_i, \hat{a}_i)$.
$\hat{\mathbf{a}}$ can be extracted from the model using gradient-

[2]We follow Wiegreffe and Marasovic (2021); Jacovi and Goldberg (2021) in referring to them as highlight explanations.

[3]An overview over NLP datasets with human explanations is provided in Wiegreffe and Marasovic (2021).

[4]For this objective, human explanations are often used as feedback in the *explanation-based debugging* setup, where a bug is identified based on a model's explanation for its prediction and fixed by correcting the model explanation (Lertvittayakumjorn and Toni, 2021).

[5]Hase and Bansal (2021) derive a framework in which some of these methods can be considered as equal.

	TASK								MODEL						EX. TYPE			METHOD					RESULTS			
Authors	DOC. CLS.	SENTIMENT ANALYSIS	HATE SPEECH	REL. EXTRACTION	MULTI CHOICE QA	NATURAL LANG. INFERENCE	EXTRACTIVE QA	OTHER	LOGREG	NAIVE BAYES	SVM	CNN	LSTM	PRETR. TRANSFORMER	HIGHLIGHT	FREE-TEXT	SEMI-STRUCTURED	REGULARIZATION	DATA AUGMENTATION	MTL	I→EX;EX→O	OTHER	OUT-OF-DOMAIN	EFFICIENCY	BIAS REDUCTION	MODEL EXPLANATION
Godbole et al. (2004)	■										■				■							■		▲		
Zaidan et al. (2007)		■									■				■							■		▲		
Zaidan and Eisner (2008)		■													■							■		▲		
Druck et al. (2009)								■							■							■		▲		
Small et al. (2011)		■									■				■							■		▲		
Settles (2011)	■														■							■		▲		
Kulesza et al. (2015)	■									■					■							■		▲		
Zhang et al. (2016)	■											■			■						■			▲		▲
Bao et al. (2018)		■												■	■							■	▲			
Zhong et al. (2019)		■											■		■			■						▲		•
Liu and Avci (2019)			■									■			■			■						▲	▲	
Strout et al. (2019)		■										■			■			■						▲		▲
Rieger et al. (2020)		■											■		■			■							▲	
Stacey et al. (2022)						■								■	■			■					▲	▲		
Carton et al. (2021)	■				■	■								■	■						■			▲		▲
Mathew et al. (2021)			■												■			■							▲	•
Antognini et al. (2021)								■						□	■					■				▲		▲
Pruthi et al. (2022)		■					■							■	■			■		■				▲		
Srivastava et al. (2017)	■								■	■						■						■		▲		
Hancock et al. (2018)				■					■							■			■					▲		
Wang et al. (2020)		■		■									■			■			■					▲		
Lee et al. (2020)		■		■				■					■		■	■			■					▲		
Ye et al. (2020)							■							■			■		■					▲		
Murty et al. (2020)				■										■		■						■		▲		
Yao et al. (2021)		■	■											■			■		■				▲	▲	▲	
Camburu et al. (2018)						■							■			■				■	■		•	•		▲
Rajani et al. (2019)					■									■		■					■		•	▲		▲
Kumar and Talukdar (2020)						■								■		■					■		▼	▲		▲
Zhao and Vydiswaran (2021)						■								■	■	■					■				•	

Table 2: An overview over methods for learning NLP tasks from highlight (upper part) and free-text explanations (lower part). The target task (TASK), model (MODEL), explanation type (EX. TYPE), and integration mechanism (METHOD) used in the respective work is indicated as ■. □ indicates a transformer model without pre-training. For results reported in the respective paper (RESULTS), we explicitly mark an observed increase (▲), decrease (▼), or minimal change ($<1\%$, •) in the evaluated quantity compared to a baseline without access to explanations.

based or perturbation-based attribution methods (Atanasova et al., 2020), or attention scores (Bahdanau et al., 2015). Intuitively, the model is forced to pay attention to input elements that are highlighted in the highlight explanation. This method is particularly suited for explanation-based debugging, as a user can directly interact with a model by modifying the highlight explanations provided by the model.

Semantic parsing to obtain noisy labels This is the dominant approach for learning from free-text explanations. The information contained in the free-text explanations is made accessible via a semantic parser that maps e to one or more labeling functions λ_i: $\mathcal{X} \rightarrow \{0, 1\}$ (Ratner et al., 2016). λ_i is a logical expression executable on input sequence $\mathbf{x}$ and evaluates to 1 if $\mathbf{e}$ applies to $\mathbf{x}$, and 0 otherwise. The set of all labeling functions is then used to assign noisy labels to unlabeled sequences for augmenting the training dataset. Existing methods differ in how the labeling functions are applied to assign noisy labels, e.g. by aggregating scores over multiple outputs or fuzzily matching input sequences. The approach hinges on the availability of a semantic parser, but several works suggest that using a relatively simple to adapt rule-based parser is sufficient for obtaining decent results (Hancock et al., 2018). Table 2 refers to this approach as DATA AUGMENTATION.

Multi-task learning In the multi-task learning (MTL) approach (Caruana, 1997), two models M_{CLS} and M_{EXP} are trained simultaneously, one for solving the target task and one for producing explanations, with most of their parameters being shared between them. When learning from highlight explanations, M_{EXP} is a token-level classifier trained to solve a sequence labeling task to predict the sequence of attributions $\mathbf{a}$. For learning from free-text explanations, M_{EXP} is a language generation model trained to generate the $\mathbf{e}$.

Explain and predict This method was introduced explicitly to improve interpretability of the model, rather than learning from human explanations to improve the target task (Lei et al., 2016). The idea is to first have the model produce an explanation based on the input instance (I→EX), and then predict the output from the explanation alone (EX→O), which is meant to assure that the generated explanation is relevant to the model prediction. The approach can be used for both learning from highlight and free-text explanations.[6] In contrast to the other methods described previously, explain and predict pipelines require explanations at test time. The human explanations are used to train the I→EX component, which provides the EX→O component with model explanations at test time.

Comparative studies We found almost no works that empirically compare approaches for learning from explanations across integration methods or explanation types. Pruthi et al. (2022) compare MTL and REGULARIZATION methods for learning from HIGHLIGHT explanations. They find that the former method requires more training examples and slightly underperforms regularization. Stacey et al. (2022) evaluate their REGULARIZATION method for both HIGHLIGHT and FREE-TEXT explanations. Results are similar for both explanation types, which might be due to the fact that explanations are from the E-SNLI dataset, where annotators were encouraged to include words contained in the highlight explanation into their free-text explanations.

2.2 Information content

Besides the choice of method for integrating explanation information, another important factor affecting model performance relates to the information contained in the explanation. Ideally, we could define specific criteria that determine if an explanation is useful for solving a task, and use these criteria for selecting or generating the most beneficial explanations, e.g. as part of annotation guidelines for collecting explanation annotations. In the following, we summarize findings of recent works that provide insights for identifying such criteria.

Selecting informative explanations Based on experiments with an artificial dataset, Hase and Bansal (2021) conclude that a model can be improved based on explanations if it can infer relevant latent information better from input instance and explanation combined, than from the input instance alone. This property could be quantified according to the metric suggested by Pruthi et al. (2022), who quantify explanation quality as the performance difference between a model trained on input instances and trained with additional explanation annotations. Carton et al. (2021) find that models can profit from those highlight explanations which lead to accurate model predictions if presented to the model in isolation. Carton et al. (2020) evaluate human highlight explanations with respect to their comprehensiveness and sufficiency, two metrics usually applied to evaluate the quality of model explanations (Yu et al., 2019), and observe that it is possible to improve model performance with 'insufficient' highlight explanations. In addition, they find that human explanations do not necessarily fulfill these two criteria, indicating that they are not suited for identifying useful human explanations to learn from. As the criteria listed above depend on a machine learning model, they cannot completely disentangle the effects of information content and how easily this content can be accessed by a model. This issue could be alleviated by using model-independent criteria to categorize information content. For example, Aggarwal et al. (2021) propose to quantify the information contained in a free-text explanation by calculating the number of distinct words (nouns, verbs, adjectives, and adverbs) per explanation.

Explanation type The works described above focus on identifying informative instances of explanations of a given explanation type. On a broader level, the information that can possibly be contained in an explanation is constrained by its type. Highlight explanations cannot carry information beyond the importance of input elements, e.g. world-knowledge relevant to solve the target task, or

[6] Wiegreffe et al. (2021) provide a recent survey on explain and predict pipelines. For space reasons, the I→EX;EX→O approaches for learning from HIGHLIGHT explanations listed in their paper are omitted from Table 2.

causal mechanisms (Tan, 2021). Hence, free-text explanations are assumed to be more suitable for tasks requiring complex reasoning, such as natural language inference or commonsense question answering (Wiegreffe and Marasovic, 2021). While this assumption intuitively makes sense, it would be useful to more formally characterize the information conveyed in an explanation of a specific type, in order to match it with the requirements of a given target task. Tan (2021) define a categorization of explanations that might provide a good starting point for characterizing information content. They group explanations into three categories based on the conveyed information: *Proximal mechanisms* convey how to infer a label from the input, *evidence* conveys relevant tokens in the input (and directly maps to highlight explanations), and *procedure* conveys step-by-step rules and is related to task instructions. With respect to matching requirements of a given target task, Jansen et al. (2016) describe a procedure for generating gold explanations covering specific knowledge and inference requirements needed to solve the target task of science exam question answering, which might be transferred to other tasks for generating informative explanations.

2.3 Human factors

Providing explanations instead of just label annotations requires some overhead from the user, which might negatively affect them. Zaidan et al. (2007) found that providing additional highlight explanations took their annotators twice as long as just providing a label for a document classification task.[7] They also point out the necessity to account for human impatience and sloppiness leading to low-quality explanations. Tan (2021) list several factors that might limit the use of human-generated explanations, including their incompleteness and subjectivity. Most importantly, they point out that we cannot expect human explanations to be valid even if the human can assign a correct label, as providing an explanation requires deeper knowledge than label assignment.

3 Take-Aways

While many approaches for improving NLP models based on highlight or free-text explanations have been proposed, there is a lack of comparative studies across different explanation types and integration methods that could reveal the most promising setup to proceed with. Initial studies on the relation between explanation properties and effect on model quality suggest that the explanation's information content plays a central role. We see a promising avenue in developing model-independent measures for quantifying information content, which could be used to give annotators detailed instructions on how to generate an informative explanation that can benefit the model, or to filter out invalid explanations that could harm model performance.

[7]We hypothesize that writing a free-text explanations might take longer than marking highlights for a given task, but could not find any comparison between annotation times for both explanation types.

Acknowledgments

We thank the reviewers for their insightful comments and suggestions. The research was funded by the XAINES project (BMBF, 01IW20005).

References

Shourya Aggarwal, Divyanshu Mandowara, Vishwajeet Agrawal, Dinesh Khandelwal, Parag Singla, and Dinesh Garg. 2021. Explanations for CommonsenseQA: New Dataset and Models. In *Proceedings of the 59th Annual Meeting of the Association for Computational Linguistics and the 11th International Joint Conference on Natural Language Processing (Volume 1: Long Papers)*, pages 3050–3065, Online. Association for Computational Linguistics.

Saleema Amershi, Maya Cakmak, William Bradley Knox, and Todd Kulesza. 2014. Power to the people: The role of humans in interactive machine learning. *AI Magazine*, 35(4):105–120.

Diego Antognini, Claudiu Musat, and Boi Faltings. 2021. Interacting with explanations through critiquing. In *Proceedings of the Thirtieth International Joint Conference on Artificial Intelligence, IJCAI-21*, pages 515–521. International Joint Conferences on Artificial Intelligence Organization.

Pepa Atanasova, Jakob Grue Simonsen, Christina Lioma, and Isabelle Augenstein. 2020. A diagnostic study of explainability techniques for text classification. In *Proceedings of the 2020 Conference on Empirical Methods in Natural Language Processing (EMNLP)*, pages 3256–3274, Online. Association for Computational Linguistics.

Dzmitry Bahdanau, Kyunghyun Cho, and Yoshua Bengio. 2015. Neural machine translation by jointly learning to align and translate. In *3rd International Conference on Learning Representations, ICLR 2015, San Diego, CA, USA, May 7-9, 2015, Conference Track Proceedings*.

Yujia Bao, Shiyu Chang, Mo Yu, and Regina Barzilay. 2018. Deriving machine attention from human rationales. In *Proceedings of the 2018 Conference on Empirical Methods in Natural Language Processing*, pages 1903–1913, Brussels, Belgium. Association for Computational Linguistics.

Oana-Maria Camburu, Tim Rocktäschel, Thomas Lukasiewicz, and Phil Blunsom. 2018. e-SNLI: Natural language inference with natural language explanations. In *Advances in Neural Information Processing Systems*, volume 31, pages 9539–9549. Curran Associates, Inc.

Samuel Carton, Surya Kanoria, and Chenhao Tan. 2021. What to learn, and how: Toward effective learning from rationales. *arXiv preprint arXiv:2112.00071*.

Samuel Carton, Anirudh Rathore, and Chenhao Tan. 2020. Evaluating and characterizing human rationales. In *Proceedings of the 2020 Conference on Empirical Methods in Natural Language Processing (EMNLP)*, pages 9294–9307, Online. Association for Computational Linguistics.

Rich Caruana. 1997. Multitask learning. *Machine learning*, 28(1):41–75.

Gregory Druck, Burr Settles, and Andrew McCallum. 2009. Active learning by labeling features. In *Proceedings of the 2009 Conference on Empirical Methods in Natural Language Processing*, pages 81–90.

Bhavya Ghai, Q. Vera Liao, Yunfeng Zhang, Rachel Bellamy, and Klaus Mueller. 2021. Explainable active learning (XAL): Toward AI explanations as interfaces for machine teachers. *Proc. ACM Hum.-Comput. Interact.*, 4(CSCW3).

Shantanu Godbole, Abhay Harpale, Sunita Sarawagi, and Soumen Chakrabarti. 2004. Document classification through interactive supervision of document and term labels. In *European Conference on Principles of Data Mining and Knowledge Discovery*, pages 185–196. Springer.

Braden Hancock, Paroma Varma, Stephanie Wang, Martin Bringmann, Percy Liang, and Christopher Ré. 2018. Training classifiers with natural language explanations. In *Proceedings of the 56th Annual Meeting of the Association for Computational Linguistics (Volume 1: Long Papers)*, pages 1884–1895, Melbourne, Australia. Association for Computational Linguistics.

Peter Hase and Mohit Bansal. 2021. When can models learn from explanations? A formal framework for understanding the roles of explanation data. *arXiv preprint arXiv:2102.02201*.

Alon Jacovi and Yoav Goldberg. 2021. Aligning Faithful Interpretations with their Social Attribution. *Transactions of the Association for Computational Linguistics*, 9:294–310.

Peter Jansen, Niranjan Balasubramanian, Mihai Surdeanu, and Peter Clark. 2016. What's in an explanation? characterizing knowledge and inference requirements for elementary science exams. In *Proceedings of COLING 2016, the 26th International Conference on Computational Linguistics: Technical Papers*, pages 2956–2965, Osaka, Japan. The COLING 2016 Organizing Committee.

Todd Kulesza, Margaret Burnett, Weng-Keen Wong, and Simone Stumpf. 2015. Principles of explanatory debugging to personalize interactive machine learning. In *Proceedings of the 20th International Conference on Intelligent User Interfaces*, IUI '15, page 126–137, New York, NY, USA. Association for Computing Machinery.

Sawan Kumar and Partha Talukdar. 2020. NILE : Natural language inference with faithful natural language explanations. In *Proceedings of the 58th Annual Meeting of the Association for Computational Linguistics*, pages 8730–8742, Online. Association for Computational Linguistics.

Dong-Ho Lee, Rahul Khanna, Bill Yuchen Lin, Seyeon Lee, Qinyuan Ye, Elizabeth Boschee, Leonardo Neves, and Xiang Ren. 2020. LEAN-LIFE: A label-efficient annotation framework towards learning from explanation. In *Proceedings of the 58th Annual Meeting of the Association for Computational Linguistics: System Demonstrations*, pages 372–379, Online. Association for Computational Linguistics.

Tao Lei, Regina Barzilay, and Tommi Jaakkola. 2016. Rationalizing neural predictions. In *Proceedings of the 2016 Conference on Empirical Methods in Natural Language Processing*, pages 107–117, Austin, Texas. Association for Computational Linguistics.

Piyawat Lertvittayakumjorn and Francesca Toni. 2021. Explanation-Based Human Debugging of NLP Models: A Survey. *Transactions of the Association for Computational Linguistics*, 9:1508–1528.

Frederick Liu and Besim Avci. 2019. Incorporating priors with feature attribution on text classification. In *Proceedings of the 57th Annual Meeting of the Association for Computational Linguistics*, pages 6274–6283, Florence, Italy. Association for Computational Linguistics.

Binny Mathew, Punyajoy Saha, Seid Muhie Yimam, Chris Biemann, Pawan Goyal, and Animesh Mukherjee. 2021. Hatexplain: A benchmark dataset for explainable hate speech detection. *Proceedings of the AAAI Conference on Artificial Intelligence*, 35(17):14867–14875.

Shikhar Murty, Pang Wei Koh, and Percy Liang. 2020. ExpBERT: Representation engineering with natural language explanations. In *Proceedings of the 58th Annual Meeting of the Association for Computational Linguistics*, pages 2106–2113, Online. Association for Computational Linguistics.

Danish Pruthi, Rachit Bansal, Bhuwan Dhingra, Livio Baldini Soares, Michael Collins, Zachary C. Lipton, Graham Neubig, and William W. Cohen. 2022. Evaluating Explanations: How Much Do Explanations from the Teacher Aid Students? *Transactions of the Association for Computational Linguistics*, 10:359–375.

Nazneen Fatema Rajani, Bryan McCann, Caiming Xiong, and Richard Socher. 2019. Explain yourself! leveraging language models for commonsense reasoning. In *Proceedings of the 57th Annual Meeting of the Association for Computational Linguistics*, pages 4932–4942, Florence, Italy. Association for Computational Linguistics.

Alexander J Ratner, Christopher M De Sa, Sen Wu, Daniel Selsam, and Christopher Ré. 2016. Data programming: Creating large training sets, quickly. In *Advances in Neural Information Processing Systems*, volume 29. Curran Associates, Inc.

Laura Rieger, Chandan Singh, William Murdoch, and Bin Yu. 2020. Interpretations are useful: Penalizing explanations to align neural networks with prior knowledge. In *Proceedings of the 37th International Conference on Machine Learning*, volume 119 of *Proceedings of Machine Learning Research*, pages 8116–8126. PMLR.

Burr Settles. 2011. Closing the loop: Fast, interactive semi-supervised annotation with queries on features and instances. In *Proceedings of the 2011 Conference on Empirical Methods in Natural Language Processing*, pages 1467–1478, Edinburgh, Scotland, UK. Association for Computational Linguistics.

Kevin Small, Byron C. Wallace, Carla E. Brodley, and Thomas A. Trikalinos. 2011. The constrained weight space SVM: Learning with ranked features. In *Proceedings of the 28th International Conference on International Conference on Machine Learning*, ICML'11, page 865–872, Madison, WI, USA. Omnipress.

Shashank Srivastava, Igor Labutov, and Tom Mitchell. 2017. Joint concept learning and semantic parsing from natural language explanations. In *Proceedings of the 2017 Conference on Empirical Methods in Natural Language Processing*, pages 1527–1536, Copenhagen, Denmark. Association for Computational Linguistics.

Joe Stacey, Yonatan Belinkov, and Marek Rei. 2022. Natural language inference with a human touch: Using human explanations to guide model attention. In *Proceedings of the Thirty-Sixth AAAI Conference on Artificial Intelligence (AAAI 2022)*.

Julia Strout, Ye Zhang, and Raymond Mooney. 2019. Do human rationales improve machine explanations? In *Proceedings of the 2019 ACL Workshop BlackboxNLP: Analyzing and Interpreting Neural Networks for NLP*, pages 56–62, Florence, Italy. Association for Computational Linguistics.

Simone Stumpf, Vidya Rajaram, Lida Li, Margaret Burnett, Thomas Dietterich, Erin Sullivan, Russell Drummond, and Jonathan Herlocker. 2007. Toward harnessing user feedback for machine learning. In *Proceedings of the 12th International Conference on Intelligent User Interfaces*, IUI '07, page 82–91, New York, NY, USA. Association for Computing Machinery.

Tony Sun, Andrew Gaut, Shirlyn Tang, Yuxin Huang, Mai ElSherief, Jieyu Zhao, Diba Mirza, Elizabeth Belding, Kai-Wei Chang, and William Yang Wang. 2019. Mitigating gender bias in natural language processing: Literature review. In *Proceedings of the 57th Annual Meeting of the Association for Computational Linguistics*, pages 1630–1640, Florence, Italy. Association for Computational Linguistics.

Chenhao Tan. 2021. On the diversity and limits of human explanations. *arXiv preprint arXiv:2106.11988*.

Stefano Teso and Kristian Kersting. 2019. Explanatory interactive machine learning. In *Proceedings of the 2019 AAAI/ACM Conference on AI, Ethics, and Society*, AIES '19, page 239–245, New York, NY, USA. Association for Computing Machinery.

Ziqi Wang, Yujia Qin, Wenxuan Zhou, Jun Yan, Qinyuan Ye, Leonardo Neves, Zhiyuan Liu, and Xiang Ren. 2020. Learning from explanations with neural execution tree. In *International Conference on Learning Representations*.

Sarah Wiegreffe and Ana Marasovic. 2021. Teach me to explain: A review of datasets for explainable natural language processing. In *Thirty-fifth Conference on Neural Information Processing Systems Datasets and Benchmarks Track (Round 1)*.

Sarah Wiegreffe, Ana Marasović, and Noah A. Smith. 2021. Measuring association between labels and free-text rationales. In *Proceedings of the 2021 Conference on Empirical Methods in Natural Language Processing*, pages 10266–10284, Online and Punta Cana, Dominican Republic. Association for Computational Linguistics.

Huihan Yao, Ying Chen, Qinyuan Ye, Xisen Jin, and Xiang Ren. 2021. Refining language models with compositional explanations. In *Advances in Neural Information Processing Systems*, volume 34, pages 8954–8967. Curran Associates, Inc.

Qinyuan Ye, Xiao Huang, Elizabeth Boschee, and Xiang Ren. 2020. Teaching machine comprehension with compositional explanations. In *Findings of the Association for Computational Linguistics: EMNLP 2020*, pages 1599–1615, Online. Association for Computational Linguistics.

Mo Yu, Shiyu Chang, Yang Zhang, and Tommi Jaakkola. 2019. Rethinking cooperative rationalization: Introspective extraction and complement control. In *Proceedings of the 2019 Conference on Empirical Methods in Natural Language Processing and the*

9th International Joint Conference on Natural Language Processing (EMNLP-IJCNLP), pages 4094–4103, Hong Kong, China. Association for Computational Linguistics.

Omar Zaidan and Jason Eisner. 2008. Modeling annotators: A generative approach to learning from annotator rationales. In *Proceedings of the 2008 Conference on Empirical Methods in Natural Language Processing*, pages 31–40, Honolulu, Hawaii. Association for Computational Linguistics.

Omar Zaidan, Jason Eisner, and Christine Piatko. 2007. Using "annotator rationales" to improve machine learning for text categorization. In *Human Language Technologies 2007: The Conference of the North American Chapter of the Association for Computational Linguistics; Proceedings of the Main Conference*, pages 260–267, Rochester, New York. Association for Computational Linguistics.

Ye Zhang, Iain Marshall, and Byron C. Wallace. 2016. Rationale-augmented convolutional neural networks for text classification. In *Proceedings of the 2016 Conference on Empirical Methods in Natural Language Processing*, pages 795–804, Austin, Texas. Association for Computational Linguistics.

Xinyan Zhao and V.G.Vinod Vydiswaran. 2021. Lirex: Augmenting language inference with relevant explanations. In *Proceedings of the AAAI Conference on Artificial Intelligence*, volume 35, pages 14532–14539.

Ruiqi Zhong, Steven Shao, and Kathleen McKeown. 2019. Fine-grained sentiment analysis with faithful attention. *arXiv preprint arXiv:1908.06870*.

Author Index